STEP UP, STEP OUT,
AND SHINE

AFRICA MIRANDA

Step Up, Step Out, And Shine
Africa Miranda

13Th & Joan Publishing

WWW.13THANDJOAN.COM

13th & Joan books may be purchased for educational, business or sales promotional use. For information, please email the Sales Department at sales@13thandjoan.com.

Printed in the U.S. A.

First Printing, October 2018

Library of Congress Cataloging-in-Publication Data has been applied for.

ISBN 978-1-7324712-1-4

DEDICATION

For my late great-grandmother, Ruth Nelson, the original diva in my life.

For all who are fighting to free their mind, free their heart, and free their spirit. For everyone who believes there is more.

LUCIDITY

WE INEVITABLY BECOME THE TAPESTRY
OF OUR ACTIONS AND OUR THOUGHTS

—Africa Miranda—

DO YOU BELIEVE that a bigger, bolder version of your life exists? Is it possible that you have yet to scratch the surface of your best life? I've heard it said on many occasions that the day you decide that your life belongs to you, is also the day that you take your first real breath. I am a living testament to this, and I can attest to the fact that life can and will offer us more if we are willing to receive it. The gifts of prosperity, success, affluence, influence, and advantage are ours for the taking. You may think I'm talking about the literal and physical trappings of success, and to some degree I am. However, to truly live a bigger and bolder life means realigning your mental state, the energy that surrounds you, the people you allow in your space and the level at which you exist in the world.

If we want to aspire to a higher level, then there is no room for mediocrity in our lives. We must reject it at all costs. There is an entire universe filled with possibilities, waiting for us to take the bull by the horns and spring forward into action if we want more. Deciding to walk in your purpose and chase your dreams wildly is the tip of the iceberg. It is almost as if we become one with the universe when we subscribe to the notion that we were destined to do more, to be more. This shift in thinking is the catalyst for your new life. This is the beginning of your journey.

Over the past few years, I've acquired a substantial tribe, through social media and in my personal life. Within each group, I was being asked very similar questions about my evolution. I realized that there was something that others noticed about the manifestation of my journey, as I was strategically doing the internal work to blossom and to bask in the moments of becoming myself. Whether through DMs, emails or face to face, or when being approached at events, those same questions about my journey were always there.

As a result, I began to examine my actions more closely. These periods of strategic self-reflection helped me to recognize that I had made a very specific set of changes in both my personal and professional life. In my case, the worlds collide, almost seamlessly. I discovered that I had engaged in very specific acts that would prove to alter the course of my journey. I also discovered that the more openly I shared, and the more transparent that I became about my intentions, feelings, goals and even the nuances in my response towards the occurrences in my life, the more visible my evolution became. There was an almost unexplainable energy present in my actions that would prove to be my response to all of the questions that were presented to me. More importantly, I had gained clarity, a luxury that we can't afford not to have.

For as long as I can remember, I have always recognized the power that comes from trusting the energy within and around us. I knew that I had a message that I could no longer afford to hold inside. The universe whispered a sweet message of conviction, telling me that all that I had learned was no longer mine, it was ours. I was now to be held accountable for sharing this message of freedom with any heart and set of ears willing to listen. This message that I speak of is confirmation of the simplistic, yet profound affirmation that reinforces the idea that we lack nothing. I repeat, we lack nothing. There is no opportunity that we are not worthy of if we are willing to do the work to gain access to it.

In this digital age, we are inundated by the overflow of information. From tutorials to inspiration, politics, podcasts, music, and media, there is no lack of noise that distorts our innermost thoughts. Sometimes it is so cacophonous that we are detached from our actual thoughts. Now, more than ever, I recognize the need to find a way to use the information and experiences that I have acquired in my life to enhance my circumstance. This is true for each of us.

We all need to arm ourselves with strategies to sort through the clutter. This book and its message have been written to serve as a tool to deconstruct our thoughts and open the floodgates of life's possibilities. So why should you listen to what I have to say? From traveling the world, to reading a neverending stock of books that drive intersectional thinking and purpose, engaging in countless hours of deep thought and meditation and learning to simply hear the voice that lives inside of me; I know without question that I have acquired an innate ability to listen and channel my energy and actions to will what I want. This book is the collection of all that I have read and learned and experienced and most importantly felt with my heart and soul.

I've long pondered writing this book and how to best share the concepts that I've acquired. It is the revelation of what others have seen in me and the transformative power of what I have been blessed to witness in myself. I am a constant seeker of life-changing energy, and I aspire to greatness. It should be noted that this book was written for those who are interested in this same level of transformative power. I have poured out my heart on these pages for those who desire to reach new levels in life and those who understand that the acts of transformation and evolution are not free. Nothing worth having is without cost. There are great rewards and sacrifices for those who believe their life is meant to be more than what it currently is.

The most powerful declaration that I can make is the following: I am free. It is my greatest hope that through this book you will discover life, love and the true breadth of your power. I pray that you find the freedom that you so desire and deserve as you embark upon the transformative trek to Step Up, Step Out and Shine.

—Africa Miranda—

ACKNOWLEDGMENTS

TO EVERYONE WHO has supported me, advised me, comforted me, believed in me...this is for you.

To my publisher: Ardre Orie, thank you for being the match that lit this beautiful flame. There would be no story to tell without your guidance, patience, encouragement. I am eternally grateful.

To my family: I am the sum of all of your oh so wonderful parts. Thank you for being my best examples of love, strength, kindness and fun.

To my loving mother: You are the best example of kindness, heart and faith I could ever ask for. Thank you for meeting me halfway and for giving me my sense of humor.

To my father: I owe my sense of adventure to you. You've led such a rich and multi-layered life and it inspires me to continue writing chapters of my own. All my love.

To my Aunties: Who would I be without the influence of your strong personalities, great style, strength, beauty and love?

To my sister Maiysha: Your freedom inspires me to continue to chase my own. I Love you to life.

To my sister and brother cousins: When family becomes true friendship. I love you all and thank you for being my first and best friends.

To my sister friends, Carron, Dafina and Stefani: Our friendship has been one of my greatest joys. The love, laughter and memories need a book of their own! You all inspire me to love harder and dream bigger. Here's to the next fifteen years!

To my Anitras: How am I so fortunate to have two special friends with the same name and the same wonderful spirits? Nuka, thank you for never letting me get too far away, for making me laugh harder than anyone, and for seeing me (pink house soon come!). Nitra, thank you for all of your kindness near or far, for making me a bonus auntie and welcoming me into one of the kindest families I've ever met. Love you both more than you know.

To the Rubies: Twenty-two years of love and sisterhood. Nobody rides harder; nobody loves harder. Beta Eta None Greater.

To my Sands Erika: Thank you for being my home away from home and always making me tell the truth. You saw this way before I did. Love you to life.

To all of my friends: You love me; you check on me; you check me (hey Shannon xo!), you inspire me; you support me; you make me laugh; you frustrate me; you make me better; you hold me close (Hannah xo), you keep me safe; you are my family.

To my digital family, all of my Twitter cousins, IG fam, everyone who has supported me over the years on this journey: I share this moment with all of you. You've cheered me on and given me encouragement when I needed it this most. I love and thank you.

INTRODUCTION

NERGY IS EMITTED and absorbed. This is also true of our daily exchanges and encounters. On a daily basis, we are sending out energy and taking it back. The way that we use that energy to illuminate our lives is where our power lies. Who we are and all that we become are a result of the light that burns internally. Transformation occurs when you harness your light, renew your power, and transform your life.

Step Up, Step Out, and Shine, was written to introduce you to the absolute best version of yourself. Such an introduction is not only magical, but also evolutionary. I meet myself on a daily basis. I am learning how to be me by learning new things about what I am capable of doing and by pushing the envelope for what I believe in.

The concepts within these pages are not your typical "cookie cutter" solutions. Step Up, Step Out, and Shine was not conceived overnight. I had to take ownership of my destiny and do the internal work first before I shared anything with you. I was in search of transformation, and I am happy to say that I look forward to the process of evolution on a daily basis, we all should. The path towards greatness does not lead to a single destination, and it is a journey that we must grow accustomed to traveling daily.

This book is not about fixing anything. You'd be surprised at how many things are not broken just because you think they are, based on someone else's opinion of you. This book was written to challenge you to rethink your truths and ideals of success. This book will dare you to do something different. The "different" that I speak of is rooted in planting seeds today for the harvest that you wish to reap tomorrow and recognizing the patterns in the tapestry of events that have shaped your life and your existence.

INTENTIONALITY

*A*S OBVIOUS AS it may sound, living intentionally must be intentional. We must acknowledge
that it is not possible for us to disregard the cacophony
of the world that far too often forces us to exist within
the messaging that tells us who to be, how to act, what
to look like and with whom to align ourselves.

We are in danger of being characterized by the ideol-
ogies of a society that does not often embrace the very
essence of who we are. The result is the manifestation
of a "robotic syndrome." The thing that is most special
about the human race is that we are all different. Sub-
scribing to the thought process that we were meant to
be "carbon-copies" is detrimental to our existence. This
idea of duplication has polluted our minds through
social media, print media, the airwaves and even the

production of our thoughts. Furthermore, this "sameness" ideology leads us towards the act of comparison.

The act of comparison has the power to rob us of the individuality in which we were created. That rare essence, buried deep in the crevices of our souls, gives us perspective and allows us to interact with the world and each other differently. The quirks and idiosyncrasies that we each possess reveal the keys to unlock purpose and passion and empower us to be exactly who we were destined to be. We must heed to and preserve what makes us unique at all costs.

Over the years, I've learned through a series of trial and error that not only do we deserve to walk in the glory of the light of our destinies, we unlock happiness in its purest form when we do. If you are ready to write a new chapter in your life, turn the page. Your time is now.

TABLE OF CONTENTS

HERE'S *WHAT* TO EXPECT

IF YOU'VE GOTTEN to this point in the book, believe me when I say "it's time to get real." I don't believe for one second that you have arrived at this page to turn back now, and I most certainly have not written this book believing that you deserve anything less than excellence

My desire is for you to have information at your fingertips that you can delve into at any point in time and any juncture in your journey, that would allow you to get instant insight and become actively engaged in thought that propels you forward or to just get your entire life! If you are in the process of self-discovery, or if you have found yourself and are currently living your best life, there is something here for you. Now, let's get into it, shall we?

Step Up, Step Out, and Shine is broken into three categories with seven segments within each category. As seven is the number of completion, I resolved to create segments that were well rounded and that lead you through a complete set of thoughts. Before each section, I have included the components below to introduce you to the concept of Step Up, Step Out, and Shine:

- The Framing Thought
- The Introduction of the Theory
- The Analysis
- The Personal Testimony
- Conclusive Commentary
- Caveats
- The Final Say

It is my hope that you will be supremely blessed, every single time that your hands touch this book. May your light shine!

—Africa—

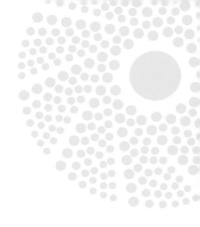

1: STEP UP

IF YOU *WANT* SOMETHING
DIFFERENT, YOU *HAVE* TO
DO SOMETHING DIFFERENT.

−Africa Miranda−

THE FRAMING THOUGHTS

WHAT WOULD WE dare to dream if we knew that we could not fail? How high would we soar if we had never been introduced to fear? The concept of stepping up is the concerted effort to change the trajectory of our lives with small, yet decisive action. Simply stated, to STEP UP is to make a decision to do something differently. So many of us think that the act of change has to be some grand gesture, but change is the most infinitesimal thought or action that can be the catalyst for manifesting our wildest dreams. Stepping up is also about ownership of the fact that our lives may not be where we want them to be because of our own shortcomings, excuses, or inability to follow-through. Finally, stepping up is about freedom. It is so rewarding to know that we possess the power to choose our thoughts that serve as electrifying energy to catapult us towards the greatest desires of our hearts. The greatest are those who understand that the way to go beyond the status quo is to recognize the connection between our thoughts and the manifestation of our actions. Effort must be exerted when one is willing to make the choice to STEP UP. Having the mindset and willingness are critical to the success of any forward movement.

THE THEORY

ASIDE FROM MAKING the decision to usher in an era of change in our lives, making the decision to take action towards said change is one of the most powerful acts in which we can engage. No matter who we are or how large our goals are, the road to achieving anything that we deem worthy of our thoughts, hopes and dreams begins with a single step. We must be compelled to take action, move forward and create progress.

WORDS HAVE NO MEANING IN THE ABSENCE OF ACTION

NOTHING WE CAN say can make the wheels turn. You are what you do, not what you say you will do. Whether we choose to admit it or not, our intentions hold no weight without the actions necessary to make them a reality. Let's have an honesty moment. Consider the opportunities that you possibly missed out on because you failed to follow up. That email you've been meaning to send but never quite got around to, the phone call you promised yourself that you would return, that date you didn't go on, out of fear or the onset of self-doubt, the trip you missed because the timing wasn't right, or the due date that you let slip by; these are all examples of motionless engagement. I was guilty of ALL of these, and I found myself being totally self-sabotaged! To be proactive means to Step Up. Whatever your soul desires will require your action and attention. Increasing productivity is often manifested in self sacrifice. Waking up an hour earlier to begin your day; or walking ten to fifteen minutes a day; or taking the stairs instead of the elevator; define ways to help us reach our personal fitness goals with added energy to put into other tasks. If you begin making one proactive choice in your life everyday, it is guaranteed that a paradigm shift will occur. The act of saying "no" to the things that don't serve us well or making a decision to not do something that we are tired of doing can free us of passive activities. It is time to make the decision to prioritize and take some action to let it go.

THE ANALYSIS

THE ACTION THAT we don't take is poison to our purpose. While I am not suggesting that we have to jump on every opportunity that crosses our paths, I am saying that when strategically orchestrated, we can benefit greatly from initiative taken towards realizing what we want for our lives. As much as we want to share our dreams, hopes and wishes with the world, none of it really matters if we are not consistently calling ourselves to action and holding ourselves accountable. Do you need an example? Why, I thought you'd never ask! How many times have we seen people prematurely make announcements about what they intend to do on "the Gram," about something that is coming, and it never actually comes? I've watched with my own eyes and scrolled with my own fingers as people hang themselves out to dry based upon a set of words. We have all been there. I get it. We are all doing the absolute best that we can, but until we disrupt our way of thinking, we will continue to have similar outcomes. Our credibility gets lost in the sauce when we speak about what will be before it actually is. Let's be clear. I don't believe for a moment that the majority of us walk around saying things that we are going to do, knowing that we have no intent to do them. It is my belief that we have every intent to move the ball forward on our goals and dreams. The fact is that the action has to be the leading actor, not the supporting cast. Consider the difference in making the announcement about an accomplishment when the work has been done, and the results are completed. The contrast is somewhat startling.

THE PERSONAL TESTIMONY

SOMETIMES THE PERSON IN
THE WAY IS YOU. MOVE!

—Africa Miranda—

THE LATE DR. Maya Angelou, in all her glory, once said that "There is no greater agony than bearing an untold story inside you." I also believe that we will never truly achieve peace and balance in our lives until we assume responsibility for the way in which our stories are told. There is tremendous power that resides within each of us, and it lives within our story. We can only unlock it once we are ready to take control of the narrative. Are you ready for a little story time?

I attended Alabama State University for undergrad, and it was all that it should have been. I had the FULL Whitley Gilbert, *A Different World* experience, and I truly blossomed during my college years. I was crowned homecoming queen, and I pledged and became a member of the illustrious Delta Sigma Theta Sorority, Inc. Even though I was very active and visible on campus, I'll let you in on a little secret: I had no idea what I really wanted to do when I graduated. My scripted response when asked about future plans was that I was going to law school. It was a perfectly respectable answer that fit the picture of where my life was, and on some level, I almost believed it. It appeared to be my next best move. Graduation came and went and so did my law school plans. I wasn't sure of my next step, but I knew it didn't lead to graduate school. Immediately after graduation and before I could stress about finding a job, I was offered a summer position from my university as a recruiter. At the end of the summer, my contract wasn't renewed, and I was out of a job. Within weeks, I was offered an appointment on the staff of the Governor of Alabama, and at twenty-one years old, I was one of the youngest appointees at the time. A few months after that, I purchased my first home, and on the surface, things appeared to be falling into place. Isn't that how life is suppose to happen? We make one decision after another that is seemingly right, and we dive in head first. Even in those moments of my life's flow, I knew that it was not what I really wanted to be doing. Why have we been conditioned to feel as though we are being ungrateful when we challenge the things that are going well? Like most, I didn't immediately; I kept going along the designated path. In retrospect, I must say that although I was making progress, I wasn't really doing anything that would embody the whole mantra of Step Up, Step Out, and Shine that I have since acquired. The real truth is that I was not pushing myself to make anything magical happen. I was caught in a web of mundane moments of time, and let me tell you, those moments don't lead to anything transformational.

A little over a year later, I received an opportunity that would turn my life upside down. At the time, I was still working in the Governor's office, but I was quietly pursuing a singing career. I worked in the studio with local producers and would drive two hours to Atlanta on the weekend to write songs and record in the hopes of being "discovered." My cousin, who was working in New York, happened to be good friends with a popular producer, and she introduced me to him. He connected me with another set of equally popular producers who were putting together a girl group. Within months, I had quit my job and moved to New York to join the group. Now, I was living in a townhouse with two girls I'd never met, a dog named Mercedes, and we were being called the next TLC. Within the first week, I was in the studio recording background vocals for Jay-Z, and over the next few months I was attending record label meetings with L.A. Reid and Tommy Mottola, and meeting 50 Cent in the studio days after he had signed his historic deal. I even met Beyonce'! (*Yes, she is that gorgeous in person and SO nice!*) To everyone back home in Alabama, it looked like I was the hometown girl who had made good. In reality, I felt like I was watching the Lifetime movie version of my life.

The producers had a very specific vision for the group...very edgy and raw. While it definitely didn't fit my Whitney Houston-esque dreams, I wanted to be a star, and if this is what I had to do to make it happen, I was down with it. I struggled with the image, with fitting in, with everything. It was also clear that one member of the production duo we were working with was not fond of me at all. I started to question everything about myself. I changed my hair, the way I dressed, and even the way I spoke. I was willing to do anything to gain his approval and to seem worthy. Thankfully, the other two girls and I got along. It was a bright spot for me during this time. One day the producer, who was NOT feeling me, was giving me a ride. I had just left a dance class and was telling him how hard I was working. He turned to me and stopped me mid-sentence and said "Look. Some people just don't have it." I was forever changed in that moment. I took that statement and made it my truth. Even today, in my dark moments, I hear him telling me those words, and I have to fight to shake it off. Shortly after this, I was replaced in the group and was left to figure out my next steps.

I didn't know what I was going to do, but I did know that I wasn't going back to Alabama. I stayed in New York for another six years with every intent to succeed, but I had no specific plans as to how to do so. Like almost every struggling artist in New York, I was recording, performing and just surviving! Let's be clear on the fact that ambition does not pay the bills, and just "getting by" can lead to burnout faster than you would think.

If I were to draw a parallel between the position with the governor and the opportunity to join the singing group, I would absolutely say that this was another example of life happening *to* me. I do believe that when you feel like throwing the towel in, the universe will send you a glimmer of hope that allows you to see the stars amidst the darkness.

A little over ten years ago, one of my sorority sisters told me about a singing competition called My Grammy Moment, and that I should enter. Mind you, this is way before online competitions were a regular thing. The contest was sponsored by Yahoo and the Grammy's, and they were looking for a singer to perform live with Justin Timberlake at the upcoming award show. You had to upload a video of yourself singing a song, and a group of industry judges would select the singers who would go on to the next round. I uploaded a video of myself singing "If I Ain't Got You" by Alicia Keys. I thought so little of this "contest" that when I realized I had sung the wrong words, I uploaded the video anyway! A few weeks later, I was notified that I had made it to the semi-final round and that our videos were going to be played on Good Morning America. People across the country had to then vote for those who would make the next round. I made it to the top five and was brought to Los Angeles for a meet, greet and press time with Justin. I performed on The Ellen Degeneres Show and was interviewed by MTV and People Magazine. The next step was another round of voting to make it to the final three. I got everyone and their mother to vote, and a month later I was being announced live during the Super Bowl. Yes, my name was announced during THE Super Bowl as one of the three finalists! Two days later, I left for Los Angeles, and I really believed in that moment that this was the start of my dreams becoming a reality. We were the "darlings" of Grammy week. This was the first time the Grammy's had ever done a contest like this; therefore, we were truly novelties. There were press events, parties, stylists, makeup artists; it was all truly a dream come true. The best moment was being able to stand on the actual stage and have a full, individual rehearsal with Justin. I had been performing for the last couple of years in New York with my own band and had overcome many of my fears that I had developed while in the girl group. I was at home on the Grammy stage and felt that I was stepping into my destiny. On the night of the show, I walked the red carpet wearing over twenty-five thousand dollars in diamonds as I rubbed shoulders with my childhood idols. We sat front row. Kanye West was to my left; Nancy Wilson was right behind me, and Prince and Ellen were just steps away. Jennifer Hudson came on stage with the envelope that held our fate. And I didn't win. I kept a smile plastered on my face because the cameras were trained on us the entire time, and I didn't want to have a meltdown in front of the entire world. I was devastated and angry!

I'm a fierce competitor, and while I was happy for the young woman who won, I WANTED TO WIN!

Days later, I was back in New York.

I often wonder and ask why are our fingertips allowed to only touch the tip of the star that we so desperately want to grab? Life happened to me yet again when I received an offer to move back down south with a friend whose family was opening a beauty boutique. I saw it as an opportunity and a possible confirmation that my dreams of entertainment were fading. Truth moment? I was so burned out that I was ready to throw in the towel. I was tired of being broke, tired of being told "no," and tired of "almost" making it. I was also starting to replay those words from that producer as a daily soundtrack. I had given up. I didn't enjoy anything about music anymore, and I tucked my tail between my legs and left New York.

When I moved to Atlanta, I was responsible for curating a buyer's experience within the four walls of the boutique. I was energized by the smell of fresh new possibilities, and I put everything into opening the store. We created something innovative and new, unlike anything that was happening in the Atlanta hair industry. The store quickly became the go-to for the city's who's who - Bravo housewives, singers, rappers, actors, reality stars all came through our doors. I was happy being close to the industry and not in it; I believed that my time had passed.

A year and a half after the store opened, a customer asked me if I modeled. At the time, I didn't know anything about commercial or lifestyle modeling. She explained that my height didn't matter and that I should check out her agency. The next week, I went to an open casting call at her agency, and I was signed on the spot. Within six months, I booked my first campaign, and the positive vibes kept on flowing. Although I had no real plan, I was fulfilled, and my life was moving forward because I was booking gigs like crazy. I guest starred on Mara Brock Akil's show, The Game, and I was featured in full page ads and on billboards for Creme of Nature and in national commercials for major brands like Curls Unleashed, Mary Kay, Discovery Channel and Verizon. Approximately three years later, I was also presented the opportunity to join a reality show on

Bravo called *The New Atlanta*. The doors of opportunity were opening, and I was tipping right on through.

On the surface, being a part of a nationally televised show was an amazing opportunity, but this was once again a gift that just fell in my lap. A close friend was initially approached to be on the show, and it wasn't a good fit for her. She presented the opportunity to me, and a year later I was starring in a reality show on one of the largest television networks in the country. My "life" was playing out publicly, but it really wasn't my story. It was a caricature; some parts true, most parts contrived for entertainment value. I look back and it's as if it all happened in some bizarre alternate universe. As much as I could, I tried to be myself; as much as anyone can in that situation. The hardest thing was accepting that people framed their thoughts of who I was based upon what they saw, and the picture was not my design. The comments on social media were crushing at times, even brutal. The startling contrast was that I actually liked where my life was at the time, and I would have much more preferred to share what I was genuinely doing at the time of filming. These shows thrive on drama, and my real life wasn't dramatic enough for prime time.

On many occasions, I can recall watching and thinking, this is not even my life.

The common thread here was that all of my actions were executed in hopes of getting chosen. Whether it was my career as a model, host, or brand ambassador, the business and my mindset at the time was that as a talent, I was awaiting opportunity. I recognize today, more than ever, that it is truly an old fashioned way of thinking, and it is counterproductive. Waiting for someone to find you really means that you are okay with not being found. To believe that someone is going to miraculously find you or that someone will give you an opportunity, and define it as being "discovered," is almost reckless. I was being well received, but by no means was I the captain of my fate. All things considered, how could I have expected for anything really special or transformational to have occured?

Let me be clear, through all that had happened, life was not bad nor was I suffering from a lack of opportunity. But that's the thing, we can not expect the opportunities that come to us to be life changing, if we are leading a passive existence. There may be good things, even great things that happen, but we won't truly reach the highest plane of our existence until we make the decision to be an active participant in our life. Life owes us nothing. We've already received life's gift; we are here, living and breathing and capable of so much. Even when you look at things on the surface, you might assume that all is well, but I promise I'm going to take you deeper. Stay with me and allow me to go there.

My wake up call dialed my number, and I answered. I recognized that I had spent much of my life just letting things happen to me. I spent almost my entire life making passive decisions. If a man liked me, I would date him. It was as simple as that. This is not to say that I ran about the town in a frenzy dating just anyone and accepting everything that came my way, but I realized that I had never sat down and asked myself what I really wanted in a partner. I had never asked myself what qualities I liked, or what I really wanted from a relationship. I was always choosing from men who had chosen me. I don't have to tell you how unfulfilling and unsuccessful that has been. I also realized that this is how most of us live. We've been conditioned to go to school, graduate, and get a job. This series of simply going through the motions based on what is expected of you is not your final destination, if you don't want it to be. I realized that the most mediocre results live, breathe, take up space, memories, and valuable time that we can never get back.

When it was all said and done, I recognized that allowing anyone other than myself to control my narrative was not how I wanted to live, and I knew without question that I needed to find a way to tell my story, my way, on my own terms. I began to rethink my voice and what I wanted the world to hear. I began to take action. That action, although minor, was symbolic of taking the initiative to Step Up.

When I became strategic about my intentions, I became more aware of my ability to rethink. Even the simple act of changing one's thoughts is proactive. To be proactive means to Step Up. It could be an act as simple as waking up an hour early to increase productivity, or walking five minutes a day or taking the stairs instead of the elevator to reach desired fitness goals. The act of saying "no" to the things that no longer serve you is a step in the right direction. If you begin making one proactive choice in your life everyday, you are embodying the affirmation to Step Up. This is the first key to abundance and empowerment.

ONE:
*W*HAT KIND OF
LION *A*RE YOU?

TELL *YOUR* TRUTH.

—Africa Miranda—

ONE OF THE things I love most about acting is the opportunity to lose myself in a character. Creating an elaborate alternate reality of sights and sounds so specific that I sometimes forget it isn't real. It also is an opportunity to learn new things about myself as I'm challenged to dig deeper each time.

You may not ever find yourself in front of a camera, but I'd like to walk you through an immersion exercise that I hope will prove to be very illuminating.

I want men to imagine themselves as a lion, and women a lioness. Let yourself stretch and see how it feels to have the wind rustling your fur, the ground beneath your sturdy paws. What do you see in the distance? Are gazelles and zebras grazing? Let out a roar and listen to it reverberate across the plain. Now close your eyes and sit with this picture for a moment.

Now when you envisioned yourself as a lion or lioness, did you see yourself as the strong king and queen of the jungle? Or did you see yourself in a cage pacing back and forth growling at little children and waiting to be fed? Both are lions, but what kind of lion are you?

I do this exercise regularly with groups and when I ask the room if they are a lion roaming free or in captivity at the zoo, ninety-nine percent of the time everyone says they are the powerful lion, free and out hunting prey. No one sees themselves as weak or not in control. But is this valid? Is how we see ourselves really the truth of who we are? In my life I was a well fed, well groomed lion. I was not roaming free, I had no real power over my life. Stepping up is rooted in honesty. Truth is the foundation on which this entire house is built. So I ask you, what is the truth? We can say all of the code words and what sounds good, but what kind of lion are we? Which one do you want to be?

Recognizing where you are is the first step. We must stop performing what we think power looks like and do the work to become authentically powerful. To Step Out, we must stop being safe and face our demons, real and imagined. This is the first step on our journey.

TWO:
THE PAST IS *A*
POWERFUL TEACHER.

YOU'RE HERE, NOT THERE.

—Africa Miranda—

IF THERE IS one thing that I know about the past, it is that it can teach us a great deal about who we are and who we hope to be. Although I don't live in the past, I do take time to reflect and assess where I am, where I'm going, and the choices and actions that have led me to this point. Many people are guilty of viewing the past in two ways: a romanticized version where events weren't "that bad," or a dark version where everything is picked apart and dissected until there is nothing positive left. I'm guilty of taking the dark version. Our true past usually lies somewhere in the middle. The key is learning to constructively study your past and take in the lessons by applying them as you move forward on your journey.

ACCEPT THAT THE PAST IS OVER

IT HAPPENED; YOU faltered. Maybe it was privately, or maybe it was publicly. Maybe, it was your fault, or maybe, you were the fallout from someone else's bad decisions or harmful actions. You have to LET IT GO. We can't live our lives frozen in amber defined by a low period or moment in our lives. Accepting your past for what it is is the first step to freedom. I spent so much time over analyzing my past while agonizing over what I could've done differently and how my life would be different if I had just made a different move. All I succeeded in doing was making myself miserable, and I halted my progress. I was so afraid of making the same mistakes of my past that I was stuck. I realized that I had to let the past be just that, the past, not my present. In the present, I was fully capable of making better decisions, and even when an inevitable misstep would come, I was armed with the knowledge of my past and able to bounce back and reset quickly.

ACCEPT THAT YOU MIGHT NOT KNOW WHAT COMES NEXT

CALLING ALL FELLOW control freaks! I know this title alone can spark anxiety. Honestly, trying to control every aspect of your life is exhausting and honestly impossible. The more we attempt to control things, the more life can potentially spiral out of control. How has it been working out for you? I was a mess. The moment I relinquished control and welcomed the element of surprise into my life, things changed. Most importantly, my perspective changed. Nothing about my life, at this moment, is what I planned or saw for myself. The beauty is that it is so much more than I could have ever fathomed. By opening your mind and spirit to being led down an unknown path, you open the door to life altering experiences and opportunities. Embracing the things that we cannot control can be the difference between living and simply existing.

RELINQUISH GUILT

HOW MANY TIMES have we replayed incidents in our mind, only to be filled with crippling regret and anger at our our past? We are so much more than the decisions we made when we were trying to figure it out. If we had had all of the answers at the beginning, chances are that we might have never stumbled upon the glorious feat that we refer to as purpose. If no one has ever said this to you, allow me to be the first. There are moments in your past that no longer reflect who you have become. This is true for me and true for all of us. I have done things that I am ashamed of and that I would give anything to change, but I've had to forgive myself. We deserve so much more than to hold ourselves hostage for parts of our past that we would handle differently today. You are not who you were. With every passing moment, we grow, evolve, and life introduces us to a new perspective. Perspective is what guides our decision making process and serves as the measuring stick for how we will address the new moments that we encounter.

OWN THE WINS

WHEN WAS THE last time you stopped to congratulate yourself? It is possible that it's been a while. Chances are that you've been working so hard, chasing goals, that you haven't realized just how far you have come. We are all guilty of it. You deserve to be celebrated, and the best person to do it is you. We are placing so much pressure on ourselves to be and to do everything, and we often forget the fact that we are winning in many aspects of our lives. The beauty of social media is that it connects us in ways we never would have imagined. The curse is now everyone has the ability to share one's best and brightest moments. In comparison, one can be left feeling less than when looking at your own accomplishments. As a result, many of us devalue our wins because they seem too small. Celebrate taking the smallest step if it is one that leads you closer to your purpose.

CLAIM FREEDOM

IF YOU DON'T believe that you are free, you are bound. Bondage comes in many different forms. We can be bound by finances, relationships, past traumas and pain points, work, goals and even dreams. We can also be bound by societal norms and pressures. One of the most harmful kinds of bondage we can experience, however, is the one that we impose upon ourselves. It must be avoided at all costs. It is so dangerous because we often don't even realize how we are holding ourselves hostage by virtue of our thoughts. How many of us have beat ourselves about not being where we "should" be based on our age? Or worse, how many of us have settled for relationships or jobs because everyone around us said that it was time? I challenge everyone reading this book to RETHINK. Take all the messaging you've received in this life about what you should be doing, how your life should look, how you should live, who you should love, and challenge every single one of them. Imagine what your life could be like if you made decisions based on what your heart truly desired instead of out of fear of breaking with the norm. Many of you reading this book can pinpoint people you know who live their lives on their own terms. Usually they are referred to as a "free spirit." More often than not, this description isn't given as a compliment. This is because a person who dares to live freely challenges the societal norm and makes the rest of the "herd" uncomfortable. The road to freedom isn't an easy one, and it takes a lot of reflection and self-work to break the chains of respectability and programming we have received.

RECOGNIZE THAT LIFE IS A PROCESS

ANYTHING WORTH HAVING takes time. This is also true of a life filled with transformation. The journey to our higher selves is one that is lifelong. We are conditioned to go through life checking off milestones and quickly moving on to the next. We graduated, check. We have a respectable job, and a respectable mate, check, check. All of the necessary material trappings are in place, check. This check off process continues until our time in this realm is done. So many of these markers are material and external, and from a young age, we're pushed to achieve them. We are often intune with what we want our lives to look like and where we want our final destination to be, but we forget to consider the process that we will have to go through to get there. By rushing to get from one stage to the next, we risk missing the lessons in between. The beauty of taking our time to be present and be an active participant in our lives means that we get to enjoy how it all unfolds. Each cycle is meant to expose our layers and push us towards new versions of ourselves.

PAY ATTENTION

OUR PAST CAN be our most powerful teacher. Bad breakups teach us how to be better partners, professional missteps reveal how to be more prepared. It's not easy to rehash painful parts of our past, but it can prove to be some of the best education we receive. Our past isn't the only place that holds valuable information. Every interaction that we experience on this earth can direct our next steps if we keep our minds and spirits open and available to receive the messaging. I challenge you to be purposeful by going through your day with a heightened awareness of the people around you, how they interact with each other and how they interact with you. One of my favorite past times is people watching. Catching the quiet moments that many miss has given me a greater appreciation for humankind. Not only do I appreciate our struggles but I also appreciate our triumphs.

THREE:

THE GREAT DETOX:
ALLEVIATING FAILURE, INFERIORITY
COMPLEXES AND OTHER DRUGS

I HAVE FAILED, BUT I AM NOT A FAILURE.

—Africa Miranda—

FAILURE IS A dangerous word. I don't subscribe to the belief that we should assume ownership of it. Each time we don't achieve the desired results for which we strive, we are presented with another opportunity to learn and stretch ourselves in new ways. It is in this space that we have open access to the abundance that we all seek. No matter how badly we want more from life, it will never happen if we are unwilling or deem ourselves unable to pursue unchartered territory, which requires us to leave our comfort zone.

If I could wave my magic wand, I would remove the word failure from all of our vocabularies. There is no moment more powerful than one that presents the opportunity to push boundaries and challenge the synergy of our words and actions.

TO SUCCEED, YOU MUST EXPERIENCE MILESTONES THAT DON'T MIRROR SUCCESS

ACCEPTING FAILURE AS a critical part of the process eliminates unnecessary hardship and grief over what did not go well. The most important aspect of what could be seen as failure is the lesson that resides in the heart of the disappointment. Pinpointing the lessons, learning curves, and even the blessings can be a very meaningful and engaging act.

Are you ready for storytime again?

One of my greatest lessons regarding failure happened in Atlanta. I was experiencing success creatively and professionally while regularly booking national commercials and print campaigns. I got an audition for a musical production that was being produced; I had a fantastic audition. I felt like this was going to be a great break for me. It involved music (yay!), and I had grown up performing in musical theatres, so I felt this was meant to be. At the first table read, I found out that I hadn't been cast in the role for which I had auditioned. Instead, I was cast as a "swing." For those of you not familiar with musical theatre, the "swing" is someone who has to cover multiple roles in the show and essentially learn the entire production. At the first rehearsal, I knew I was in over my head. Normally, a production like this takes six weeks or more to launch; however, this production was being launched in two weeks. I struggled with connecting with the four characters I had to cover and the choreography. I struggled with everything, and the more I fell behind the more my self-confidence plummeted.

Around the fourth day, the director started firing actors that weren't meeting the expectations in rehearsal. His reasoning was that they didn't have time to prepare actors; they needed actors who could jump right in and excel. I felt ill because I feared I would be the next to be fired, and I was praying I was next because it would end the misery. I was so off my game at this point I couldn't even do simple eight counts. It had become daily practice that firing happened at lunchtime. Before the cast would break for lunch, the director would call out a set of names, and they would be sent home. By the seventh day, lunchtime came and sure enough my name was called. The director took me and another actor into his office and let us go. I was mortified. I let my ego tell me I was a working actor and model who could sing. This shouldn't be happening to me, but I was also relieved. I was dying in those rehearsals. I went home and licked my wounds for the night. The next day I had to face the truth of what had happened. My firing was totally justified. My talent wasn't in question, but my work ethic definitely was. Acting scares me. It's the part of my craft that has always come the hardest because I am an overachiever. I avoided the hard parts of studying because I didn't like feeling as if I weren't the "best" at something. I could book commercials and modeling campaigns like clockwork, but dramatic roles or projects like this play proved that I was out of my depth. I resolved in that moment to face the truth, accept the shame of what had happened, and do the work so that it never happens again. In that moment, I totally failed, but I didn't let that failure define my career.

VALIDATION IS FOR PARKING

WE ALL HAVE the need for validation. There is no way around this yearning. We deserve to know that we are okay. There is no harm in wanting and getting reassurance in who we are and the work that we do. The key is recognizing that when we are in the pursuit of greatness, it will require more attempts than the average person is willing to make. Stepping up means that you are pushing past barriers to move outside of the norm into a new realm of possibilities. Pushing past barriers also means an adjustment in the way we seek validation which will prove beneficial as we embody the concept of stepping up.

GET MAD

TO PRETEND THAT frustration does not exist during the cultivation process is equivalent with being out of touch with reality. Failing, not winning, is one of the most daunting parts of the process. Anyone who feels is also likely to hurt from the experience. The good news is that, it's okay and should be considered a part of the process. Although super uncomfortable, the process of channeling anger and disappointment can eventually bring comfort. Go ahead and get frustrated and get mad, but remember to pick yourself up and pat yourself on the back. I'm very competitive, and I love winning and being chosen. When I don't reach a goal or I'm not chosen for an opportunity, I get "BIG" mad. There's nothing wrong with a little "fire" or competitive edge to push us past complacency. I believe in acceptance, but it should never dampen one's spirit. Are you feeling embarrassed? If so, that is good! It's time to get to work and make sure that it doesn't happen again!

FALL FORWARD AND FAST

IF YOU ARE going to fall, you might as well use the momentum to make it as quick and as painless as possible. No one benefits from failing slowly. Go down in a blaze of glory! At least you are in the game and trying. I took a professional risk last year that failed miserably. I spent most of 2017 working the tenets of this book to get myself back on track. In fact, my main solace was writing this book. If I were going to say it, I truly had to live it. While you are down, get the most out of it. Figure out how you got there and then figure out how to get back up. Determine how much time it will take you to do so. Plot that ascension and keep in mind that if you are indeed down, then the beauty is that you can't get any lower!

THE END. NEXT CHAPTER.

YOU HAVE TO let it go, boo! Feelings of failure have this unprecedented power that somehow takes hold of us and tells us that we are not good enough for what we want or what we are trying to do. The voice of distress ends up silencing the voice of reason. Once you've identified the failure, recognize it and move on. You are the author of your story, which means that you have control. Your current failure can either be a short story or your four hundred page memoir. It is a part of your life, but it doesn't define you. Accepting

STEP UP. STEP OUT. AND SHINE

that failure will happen repeatedly in our lives takes its power away. Failure is not a surprise, nor will it disrupt your life. Failure is merely a footnote at the bottom of the page. This is the end of a chapter, and the beginning of a beautiful new beginning, if only you believe.

THROW OUT THE JUDGE AND JURY

IF WE WERE honest, we would admit that the opinions of others is a considerable factor in why we do what we do. We perform for the applause from others. To be told "I'm proud of you" to adopting the goals that others believe we should be achieving reflect our deep desire to be accepted and made worthy by the standards of others. We have a strong desire to avoid the scrutiny and judgment of others; therefore, we cling to the opinions and perceptions of those around us. Constantly angling for acceptance leaves us no time to figure out what we really want. At one point in our lives, each of us has been subjected to the judge and jury. Insight from those around us can be helpful, but we have to consider the source. In this initial phase of self-discovery, understand that there may not be many in your circle who understand or even support your new path. How can others advise you if they have no frame of reference for where you're going? I've learned that there are people in my life who can give me love, but not advice. Constantly seeking affirmation from people ill equipped to give it to you is unfair to both of you. The journey to your higher self is frequently a solo trip. Work to quiet the need for a fan club and learn to self-motivate. When we are left to sort through thoughts about ourselves and reflect on how far we have come or how far we have left to go, we are better positioned to win.

GET VISUAL

JUST BECAUSE YOU didn't succeed according to your terms doesn't mean that the goal gets tossed out of the door. Visualizing yourself winning at whatever you opt to do must be a part of the process. It is often said that athletes who are most successful have mastered the art of visualizing themselves running across the finish line. If you don't compose the vision of how it all should be, what then are you aiming for? Vision boards have played a huge role in helping me to craft a clear vision for my life. Every year, I create a new one, and it has a specific theme. Having a theme is important because your vision needs connective tissue. The words and images I select aren't merely a collage, but they form an intricate tapestry that tells the story I hope to see for the year to come. I also make a secondary, digital, vision board that is the lock screen on my phone that I see multiple times a day, and it is a conscious and subconscious reminder of what I want to manifest in my life. Your ability to visualize is not a guarantee that everything will go according to plan, but it does dare you to dream. As we get older, we stop fantasizing because we're advised that it's time to grow up and live in the real world. Visualization is so powerful because it taps into our inner child and wakes up that part of us that has been sedated by the minutiae of everyday life.

FOUR:

REJECTION: NO IS A NEW BEGINNING

REDIRECTION IS A GIFT FROM THE UNIVERSE.

—Africa Miranda—

J UST BECAUSE YOU want it, does it mean that you are supposed to have it? For so many, the beloved grind is alive and well. There has definitely been a surge in the opinion that if we believe we should have something, it will inevitably belong to us. The problem with this train of thought is that rejection is inevitable, and if we frame every scenario as having "haters" or some other reason that takes the onus off of us, then where is the lesson? This may be an unpopular thought, but are we truly supposed to have everything we want? When we resolve to STEP UP, we discover that rejection is a blessing in disguise, as it becomes a roadmap that directs us towards destiny.

Addressing rejection and the feelings that we associate with it is the first step towards shifting our thoughts and assuming the hidden power of it all. The discussion of overcoming rejection is not for the faint of heart, but it is necessary if we want to reach a level of excellence in our lives. A person who is fine with not challenging the status quo isn't going to analyze rejection or examine steps necessary to push through all of the no's. These truths will only resonate with those who are ready to push past being average. Could that be you?

ASK YOURSELF THE HARD QUESTIONS

HAVE YOU DONE the work, or have you been getting by on a wing and a prayer? Are you really up to par? Are you as deserving of the opportunities that you seek as you believe that you are? There are moments in life that are disguised as opportunities that result in rejection. And in those moments, it is easy to question everything and everyone except yourself. The most significant demonstration of growth is taking full responsibility for what does or does not manifest in your life. We must ask ourselves in the heat of rejection the following question: "What have I done that really matters?" One of my most embarrassing professional moments was getting fired from a job I wasn't prepared for. That was a pivotal moment for me because in that moment I accepted the truth: I had been getting by. I promised myself in that moment that I would honor my gifts and any future opportunities that I received by doing the work on my craft. On the quest to STEP UP, and discover the light that we have the opportunity and ability to walk in, we must seek nothing less than excellence. A part of this process is feeling the bumps and bruises of life that come with rejection.

FIND THE LESSON

WHEN WE ARE rejected, who is responsible? It is easy to identify the people and factors outside of our control as the root causes, but when we are rejected, the message we are receiving from the universe is to look inward. To analyze your rejection and recognize and accept responsibility for the part you played in it can sting. We have to shelve our egos and stand in the uncomfortable truth that is the fact that the rejection may have been justified. Let's not forget however, that there are some instances where it is possible that you did all that you could do. Maybe you WERE attentive to the things that were within your control and maybe you DID do all the work. In those moments, rejection must be viewed as an opportunity to learn acceptance, humility, and perseverance. There have been so many times in my life that rejection was preparation for something even greater than I had imagined. There are also times that rejection turned out to be protection from situations that would have damaged me personally, professionally and emotionally. That girl group I was a part of back in the day? The rejection from that producer set me on a path to find my voice and my way in this business...ultimately leading me to the very words you're reading in this book. Never discount rejection and always be open to the lesson waiting for you.

GET PROACTIVE

A WAY TO take your power back in the face of rejection is to ask yourself what you can do differently the next time. Taking a proactive approach to rejection can reveal new discoveries. Considering measures to anticipate the series of events to follow the rejection, setting your sights on a new goal and taking time to understand the source of rejection, are all strategies. Being proactive also means not waiting for things to happen. Rejection could be the nudge from the universe to create your own platform or birth your own idea. The "no" doesn't mean that you're not capable. It may mean that you're meant to do it own your own. When you know what you want and you are working towards achieving it, there is no reason to wait. It should be noted that we all deserve moments to rest and reset. Resting is proactive as it is needed to replenish us mentally and physically to continue the work of manifesting our goals. The moments of rest could also prove to be a time to gain perspective on the redirection that can change your life.

CREATE A TOOLBOX

IF WE ARE fortunate to see another day, we will experience rejection in one way or another. It is the risk that we take for trying. There is beauty in the act of reaching for something other than what already exists and there is absolutely no shame in attempting and not achieving. The way in which we respond to rejection is just as important as how it occurs. Rejection is not the way that the story ends, if you don't allow it to be. We just have to have the necessary tools to process it in a healthy way, instead of viewing it as the end of the world every time it happens. The first step is to treat yourself with kindness. There are times when our first instinct is to berate ourselves for being rejected. You deserve better. There are so many elements that cause us strife in everyday life that we must learn to take better care. Engaging in positive self-talk and affirmations that promote self-worth and value is another tactic to avoid the negative impact of rejection. Lastly, your ability to recognize your strength can change your perspective and grant you access to newfound freedom, even when things don't go your way. It is only from a place of strength that we can attempt to achieve and set goals that place us in the line of fire. These moments will go down in history as some of the greatest moments of our lives. These moments, inevitably create the very fibers of who we are and who we are destined to become.

CHANGE YOUR IDEA OF THE FAIRYTALE

WHY IS IT that we believe that we deserve everything that we try for? The whole "I deserve" phrase is highly overrated. The truth that many are afraid to say is that we are not deserving of everything, simply because we think that we are. That idea is a fairytale and this train of thought can lead to disappointment. Dar I say that we We have to consider that we were not the best candidate for a particular opportunity. We have to consider that it was simply a matter of bad timing. We have to consider something was not necessarily aligned for us. These are all possible explanations for why the story does not always end as we say that it should. The best news ever is that we still have the power to control our responses to it all. This also means that even when we feel out of control, we can still take control of the narrative of our lives, even when rejection is present.

SHAKE IT OFF

IT IS IMPERATIVE that you ask yourself how badly you want what you are chasing? If you want something as badly as you say that you do, rejection won't stop you. I've gone on hundreds, possibly thousands of auditions over the last 10 years...have you seen me in thousands of commercials, films or tv shows? As a talent you have to get used to rejection very quickly. If you don't, you won't survive long in this business. There are so many factors at play when a performer is selected. At a certain level, everyone is talented and it becomes about the intangibles. Something as arbitrary as height or the ability to fit a costume can be the deciding factor. Knowing this has freed me from feeling worthless or questioning my ability every time I don't book a job. Try adopting this same thought process to your own rejections. When rejection happens, ask yourself if you did your best, give thanks for the opportunity to move closer to your goal, and keep moving forward.

Although at times, you may experience moments of disappointment, you will not be deterred from the very thing that your heart years for. This is also an indicator of your motives and intrinsic drive. To get something that not everyone else has, you will inevitably have to do some things that not everyone else is willing to do.

EXCELLENCE ONLY

MEDIOCRITY IS AN insult to the greatness that was created in each of us. Avoidance of mediocrity, first requires examination of the status quo.

Rejection is a clear indication that you are pushing your limits at all costs. If you ever needed proof that you were attempting to do something great, rejection makes a solid case. It is in this space, that we must learn to commend ourselves what is happening. Chances are, if you are experiencing rejection, there are many opportunities that have manifest. There is power in learning to see the value in what is. You have achieved and you will achieve again. A careful examination of our wins and losses definitively demonstrates that we have a reason to keep hope alive. If you are making decisions in your daily walk to STEP UP, mediocrity is an afterthought.

FIVE:

SELF-TALK AND AFFIRMATIVE ACTIONS

YOU ARE ENOUGH.

—Africa Miranda—

YOUR WORDS CONTROL your thoughts. What you allow yourself to speak is a clear indicator or what you will allow yourself to do. I like to think of affirmations as tools with extraordinary power. My Thor hammer if you will. Affirmations serve us in multi dimensional ways but the most important is that they counter the negative inner thoughts and outward words that we far too often use to destroy ourselves. We all do it. Whether because of something we heard, a comparison that we have made about ourselves or even past pain points, we internalize these outward messages as our inner truths. The conversation we have with ourselves is the most important because it frames how we see ourselves, how we move about in the world and how we interact with others. Understanding the power that is accompanied by engaging in self talk or affirming ourselves can only be channeled when we unlearn what society has taught us about who and what we are.

We must find a way to put affirmations to work and create a source of refuge for our minds and thoughts on a daily basis. Positive thinking and self-talk is a muscle that must be trained as if we are prepping for the Olympics. The aha moment for me was realizing that to be familiar with affirmations was not enough. I had to learn to move past just being familiar into a space of complete comfort with the act of positive self-talk. At first it can feel strange, speaking into the void. You may feel self-conscious and more than a little odd when you begin. I definitely did! Overtime it will become more natural and even a self-soothing mechanism when anxiety or stress hits.

At this point, I am certain that we are all familiar with what an affirmation is but the bigger question becomes, how do they work best in our lives? What makes the words that we speak morph into manifestations of prosperity or happiness or abundance? What changes in our psyche that allows us to believe that life has more and that we have access to the more? Moreover, can we assume that what works for one is what works for all? It is imperative that we break the habit of jumping head first into what others say is good for us. Taking time to go deeper is key. Here are a few steps that serve as an precursors to an open invitation to the power of positive self-talk and affirmations:

DENOUNCE SOCIETAL IMPOSED OBLIGATIONS AND STEREOTYPES

ARE BLACK WOMEN really angry or has society created that narrative? Are all men unfaithful, or have we been encouraged to accept that as truth? Consider other stereotypes that have been used to define your intrinsic story. Without realizing we can internalize these messages and limit how we see ourselves in the world and what we aspire to accomplish. It is so important that we are aware of these scenarios as we work to reverse their impact.

ADD A FILTER...AND A MUTE BUTTON

OVER THE YEARS, I've learned how to filter what I allow to take up space in my heart, my mind and my soul. For the sake of my sanity, I had to recognize that all messaging and all information is not worthy of my attention. Something as simple as turning off my notifications from social media has allowed me to engage in more self-talk or at the very least to not be distracted from it. Simple things like not engaging in gossip and tainted information exchanges is another example of a filter. I no longer have cable, watch much less television, and do my best to quiet the noise of life so that I am able to hear divine messages when they are sent my way.

KNOW YOUR NAME

EVERYTHING THAT IS said to us, is not ours to own. If you were walking down the street and someone called you by a name that did not belong to you, chances are, you would not answer. Why do we allow people to describe us with characteristics that do not embody the essence of who we are? Why do we own the words of others? The opinions of others can be just as harmful as they are powerful. They can impact us in both positive and negative ways. The good news is that we get to decide. The power to determine how we are moved by other people's judgement of us is ours for the taking.

CONSIDER YOUR INTERNAL GPS

WHERE DO YOU want to go? What direction will take you there? What things do you want to manifest in your life? What baggage must you drop off along the way to reach your final destination? Discovering an internal roadmap is a powerful act. We must learn to be led by our intrinsic beliefs and motivations. Far too often, we travel through life on a path dictated by others. We bend to the will of well meaning family and friends, or even our own expectations of what we think the "proper" path is. If you are reading this book then there is a good chance that you've started your journey to self-discovery. Asking the questions above will help you start to chart YOUR course, not the one laid out for you by others. Remember we are as unique as fingerprints, which means that our life's journeys will be too.

NOURISH YOUR SOUL

WHAT YOU CONSUME mentally, visually, spiritually and even recreationally, affects your ability to breathe life into your words. Just like a diet of processed food will ultimately break down the body, leaving it primed for disease, it is the same for our spirits. How can we expect to produce positive words within if we are not continually nourishing ourselves with them? A constant diet of negative thoughts, words and images won't sustain you long term. We have to proactively find ways to counteract the superficial and negative messages that surround us daily. The more that we position ourselves amidst positive vibes, the more we will embody that same spirit. Something as simple as making a playlist to listen to when we need a pick me up helps. Creating a nighttime routine that settles your mind and spirit, cleansing you of the energy you've accumulated throughout the day, can help you rest soundly at night.

OPERATE IN TRUTH

WE MUST LEARN that the truth is the light that we should seek. The culture is often so backwards that we often view the truth as harsh. This has placed us at a great disadvantage because we are programmed to believe that being honest with ourselves about things that may not be positive, somehow sets us back or makes us less than. Nothing could be further from the truth. Honesty allows us to be free. Honesty through our words, helps us to rescue them from bondage, a luxury we can't afford to live without. Operating in truth also invites honest and genuine interactions and connections into our lives. For the majority of my adult I haven't shared my real age. I've given different numbers depending on the occasion, mainly because in the entertainment business youth is king. Also from childhood I constantly heard the message from society that "a woman never tells her age." (Who came up with this? A man?) I came to realize that by living this lie I was inviting lies into my life, because my message to the universe was that I accept dishonesty. My truth also was that I didn't feel as accomplished as I should have for someone my age. I couldn't truly Step Up, Step Out, and Shine until I was ready to fully stand in the light. At 41 years old my truth is now that I am grateful for my journey, my life and for all that is still to come.

GET MENTALLY FIT

IN THE MORNING, before you begin your day, take a few moments to center yourself. Don't allow the internet to rush you. Not being the first to show up for the social media show, will in no way affect the abundance that has been promised to you. Take time to remind yourself that you are ok, as you are and you're growing. Tell yourself that you look and are fine. Proclaim that it will be a good day. These are small acts of kindness that you can give to yourself. Creating rituals that force us to slow down and honor ourselves starts our day on a positive path. We can then handle whatever we may encounter throughout the day. So much time is spent pouring into others that we often forget the details involved to pour into ourselves. We are worthy of our own time and we must make it a priority to build our mental capacity and ability to affirm at all times.

SIX:

#THEPLUG: CHANNELING YOUR POWER FROM WITHIN

THE TRUTH IS YOUR POWER.

—Africa Miranda—

T HE ONLY WAY to truly be powerful is to assume ownership of it. The truth is that the world does not have the ability to give you power anymore than it has the ability to take it away. Assuming that we are gifted an abundance of power, also means that there are no true limitations on what we can achieve or who we can become. Examining our truths about the way in which we define power is paramount to our evolution. The world has shown us so many examples of power and many of these messages we adopt as our truths. It is possible that some of the examples that we have witnessed are have not served us well. In a society that tells us to be and do more than the next person and to aspire to superficial notions of success, we must learn to assume ownership of our own definitions of power.

If we believe ourselves to be powerful, then we have access to a never ending cache from which to make withdrawals. I define power as freedom. It is simple, yet simultaneously complex. Thriving in life is freedom to live how you want, dress how you want, and speak how you want. And as much freedom that power provides, it also implies that there some elements that we must assume control of in our lives. There are factors that we must oversee, to ensure that we are rising to the occasion and answering the door, when our calling knocks.

No matter what you believe, or who you believe in, there is a larger force that guides the energy surrounding each element of your position in the world. We have been given gifts and tools and a brain and analytical thoughts for a reason. It is up to each of us to be good stewards over that which is given to us. When we are intentional in the way we spend our time, what we dedicate our energy and resources to and who we strive to become, we continue to gain access to the abundance of freedom. At the same time, we must also recognize that there are factors that pose a problem to our access to freedom. To truly live in the most powerful spaces of our lives, we must examine the factors that threaten our power. Recognizing potential threats, allows us to better prepare and devise strategies to channel our greatest power and walk in truth.

LOOK IN THE MIRROR

TRUTH MOMENT? NO one can do any damage to you that is worse than what you can do to yourself.

It is possible that your worst critic is you. We have a tendency to place so much pressure on ourselves to be who we believe that we should be rather than taking the time to notice that we are evolving. Give yourself credit for the small goals reached, they are important too. This is why self- talk and self-motivation is so important and protecting your energy and your at all costs. To love yourself, is to be powerful.

STOP WAITING

THERE IS NOTHING that can make you feel more powerful than stepping out into unchartered territory and risking your comfort zone to achieve something that your heart has desired. Stop waiting! There will never be a perfect time to do anything. You will never have every duck in a row and it is possible that you won't be able to see which stars have aligned in the distance. These are all challenges that lead us towards making the decision to wait. In these moments, we must ask ourselves, what exactly are we waiting on? Purpose is a funny thing in that it chases us. Even when we want to rest, it will not allow us to do so in peace. And when it calls, you have one job...pick up the phone.

MAKE PEACE WITH YOURSELF

YOU CAN NOT increase your power if you allow pain, hurt, grief, guild, sorrow and regret to dim your light. It is not possible to allow these forces to be active, while simultaneously channeling power within. I often say that closed fist can't receive any blessings. By holding on tightly to bad decisions and "what if's," we aren't open to grasp new opportunities, new connections and new messages the universe is trying to send our way.

PERSEVERE AND REMAIN OPTIMISTIC

WE'VE ALL HEARD the mantra "Thoughts become things." It's true. At the risk of sounding like an after school special, you CAN in fact do it if you think you can. Learning to remain in the present moment and to push through with optimism is the way. It's the grit of holding on when you can't actually see the finish line that makes you realize how powerful you are. It's easy to thrive when things are going well. The essence of who we are is how we react when our mettle is tested. And although not always comfortable, recognizing that you have the ability to discover optimism amidst the struggle is quite the feat. Success isn't always about talent and skill, most times it due to perseverance. Who was willing to stay the course, who was willing to continue after countless missteps and rejections. Visualizing yourself victorious and stretching yourself beyond any barriers that you ever even knew existed, must not be optional. Perseverance is the price that we pay for making the decision to STEP UP, and doing so is worth every bit of the investment.

FIND YOUR CENTER

WE ARE ALL different and finding a place of refuge for our emotions to air out can be challenging. It is however time well spent. To center yourself, means to reset your mind, body and soul. Everything that is responsible for output or performance must have the opportunity to recharge. Your emotions are no different. The act of grounding yourself emotionally, makes you a master of your output. From morning affirmations to quiet moments and creating self-care practices and the consistent engagement with positive affirmations, you need and deserve every opportunity to establish meaningful routines to preserve your state of mental health. There is also space for emotional healing during this time. The goal is to be present within yourself at all times.

"NO" IS ENOUGH

GIVING ATTENTION OR energy to anything that does not serve you well is not up for discussion. The more you live, the more you recognize that your time is not worth wasting under any circumstance. Denying access to the things that are not of value, especially where your time is concerned, is the ultimate power move. There are times when saying "no" also means denying yourself. Stand behind your decision to say "no." Don't renege on your choice. Own it. Make no apologies for doing what will be best for you in the long run. You may be called selfish by those around you for establishing boundaries, and here's the thing, you ARE BEING SELFISH. YOU SHOULD BE SELFISH. Society has conditioned us to believe that martyrdom equals being a good person, when in fact all it has done is made us enablers and users. Prioritizing yourself doesn't mean that you have no regard for others. By honoring yourself and your goals you establish a value system that everyone in your life has to follow. You also set a beautiful example for others that have been putting themselves last for so long and are looking for inspiration to change.With a healthier mindstate, you gain more access to your power from which to help, guide or be of service to others.

SIT IN THE DIRECTOR'S CHAIR

ON A SET, the director is the ultimate ruler. He or she calls the shots, no one moves unless they say so, and the project we all get to see is the result of their meticulous vision. This is the approach we all must take with our lives. The power to tell our own story rests solely in our own hands and we must fight for ownership at all costs. Until you own your own story, you can't be free. Every ounce of the power that you need, resides in you. Right now, in this very moment, you have exactly what you need. Taking ownership of the story of your life places you in the director's chair. This is *your* story to tell. The plot twists and the nuances of the things happening around you, make the story worth telling. Choosing how you will respond to life and taking a proactive approach in doing so is never a bad thing. What if we recognize that our power is regenerated inside? What if we challenged the idea that we needed external forces to make us powerful? Not doing so, leaves us enslaved to elements that diminish our light. We can't' wait for the world to validate our worth, oru power or our worthiness. Knowing that you are all that you are and all that you should be is the final say.

SEVEN:

LET FREEDOM RING: LIVING ON YOUR OWN TERMS AND DENOUNCING THE NEED FOR PERMISSION TO DO SO

THIS IS THE SEASON FOR LIBERATION.

—Africa Miranda—

WE ARE DRIVEN by both emotions and intelligence. Both are factors in who we become and what we believe about ourselves. Living on our own terms commands that we maintain a healthy balance between what we feel and what we think. There is no proven right or wrong way to live. There is no path that is one size fits all. The terms of engagement for each of our lives are different. Embracing this notion empowers us to not only determine who we are but also to denounce who the world wants us to be. The saying: "Don't let the internet rush you" is about as real as it gets. The act of comparison leads us along undesirable paths when we are trying to construct our views of the world. When we resolve to become our own judge and jury, we also resolve to become our own measuring stick for success. Learning to stand alone, with your opinion and your vision, in the midst of what you want and will for your life is a practice that must be discovered on an individual basis.

Living according to your own terms also means that you have taken the time to learn about yourself, and you have done the work to discover what makes you happy. Achieving freedom in our lives means that we have recognized the importance of telling the negative committee that meets inside of our heads, to sit down and give it a rest. Most importantly, letting go of the need for permission from others to live our best lives is a process that we often forfeit. What others think of you is their choice and often times has very little to do with you. What you believe about yourself has every-thing to do with the reflection staring back at you in the mirror.

BUILD A LIFE THAT MAKES YOU FEEL PROUD

WHAT IS YOUR greatest source of sunshine? How do you create your own happiness? Building a life that you are proud of begins with being proud of who you are as a person. It is possible to grow accustomed to taking cues about happiness and fulfillment from outside sources. We all fall victim to this at one point or another. The need to be understood, coupled with our desire to be loved and accepted, often make us fail to recognize that there is an infinite storage of happiness that can and must be cultivated within. Take time to acknowledge the things of which you are most proud and recognize that you have overcome some things to be where you are in this present moment. Acknowl-edge the progress that you have made and embrace the journey that you are preparing to embark upon.

The simple fact that you are still standing means that you have lived to tell the story, and that alone should prompt feelings of being proud of yourself.

INVEST IN YOURSELF

GIVE YOURSELF PERMISSION to be a masterpiece and a work in progress simultaneously. If no one has ever told you, do know that you are allowed and encouraged to still be learning. Your age and where you are on your journey do not matter. Continuous progress is the name of the game, and a commitment to being a lifelong learner is critical to your ability to break through and ascend to higher heights. When you take the time to invest in yourself, you stand to gain a much larger return than the minimal risk that initial investment required. There are no limits to how you can invest in yourself. You ___ ___ a foreign language, set and work towards pers ___ ___ orga- nizations that spark you ___ venture to see the world ___ ative for you to invest ___ for the taking.

CONNECT *WITH* SOMETHING
OR SOMEONE

A DETRIMENTAL MISTAKE that we often make is attempting to "do" life alone. This is not to say that there are specific rules and guidelines about who we involve in our lives, but what is irrefutably true is that our souls yearn to connect with something outside ourselves. Living our lives online and surviving on digital connections alone, have turned most of us into accidental hermits. We were not meant to live in isolation. Even for the most significant introvert, the human connection must be satisfied. Living in self-imposed isolation does not allow us to gain access to new ideas and patterns of thinking that assist us in the quest to STEP UP.

CONSIDER *A* PERSONAL
MISSION ST*A*TEMENT

IF YOU CAN define who you are, you can define where you are headed. In life, our goal must not be to simply survive but to also thrive amidst evolving into the best versions of ourselves. Who are you? What do you want to be your legacy? What motivates you? What is your goal? What is your purpose? These are all questions that we should ask ourselves on a continual basis. Taking care to note that the answers to these questions can and should evolve. Evolution that is both meaningful and intentional is at the crux of personal development.

EMBR*A*CE *WHAT* IS DIFFERENT

HAVE YOU EVER stopped to consider that imperfection is a gift? If you've managed to discover that thing that sets you apart from the crowd, it's time you uncovered it. Remember the times that you wanted nothing more than to fit in? Those days are long gone, and if they are not, they should be. Knowing what makes you special is an opened door to acceptance of self. We are all laced with imperfections, flaws and wonderful quirks that are specific only to us. The moment when we realize that our only objective and purpose is to inspire others, is the moment we also recognize that we don't need to be perfect to do so. The way in which we handle our imperfections speaks the loudest about who we are. What we have managed to overcome and the way we handle trials and tribulations demonstrate to the world that we are human.

STOP APOLOGIZING

OWN IT. OWN all of it. We must learn to stop omitting pieces of ourselves to appease others. At some point, we can recognize that those who truly love and respect us for who and what we are, will remain present in our lives. Those who exit were likely never truly accepting of us from the beginning. As much as we all want to be liked, the unfiltered truth is that everyone will not find you favorable. You will not be the favorite or "chosen one" in every scenario. There will be times when the stars just aren't aligned in your favor. It happens. Every time isn't your time. These are facts. In spite of it all, you've got to be you anyway. At no point should your self-worth be contingent upon the opinion of others. The more that we can condition ourselves to take cues from the depths of our souls, the more we can discover that authenticity doesn't demand apology.

MAKE PEACE WITH THE PAST

NOTHING WHISPERS IN our ear more than the past, and those whispers will continue until we replace that voice with the present and the future. You can't build an elevated, internal infrastructure if you haven't constructed a solid foundation. Past attempts that didn't yield the intended results, past trauma, past childhood pain, past hurt and past feelings of rejection are more powerful than we sometimes acknowledge them to be. The absolute best part of making the decision to move forward with our lives is that we have the power to reprogram our minds to recognize and listen to affirmations about our future goals. By openly acknowledging our past, specifically the parts we want to run from the most, we release the power it holds over us. We can then harness that power to propel us on the new journey to our higher selves.

THE
FINAL SAY

TO BE *WILLING* IS NOT
ENOUGH. *WE* MUST DO.

—Africa Miranda—

CAVEATS AND FANCY THINGS:
ALL THINGS *WORK* TOGETHER

PURPOSE IS DISCO*V*ERING
SOMETHING *W*ORTH LI*V*ING FOR.

—Africa Miranda—

PART OF MY purpose is sharing my story. And I must admit that at times, it gives me butterflies. Bearing your soul and being vulnerable to the world is not for the faint of heart, but there is great value in doing so. The layer of transparency that frightens you the most, proves time and time again that you had a purpose before anyone had an opinion.

Over time, I have come to recognize that sharing my journey is a significant part of my quest to be of service to others. Walking in truth and helping people to learn from my life and my experiences are the ultimate fulfillment of my calling. I've received confirmation in so many ways and on so many occasions that my greatest reward would come from transferring all that I have learned to help others aspire to live their best lives.

In recognizing this purpose, it has become crystal clear to me that the things that happen to us are not a random series of events. There is a definite reason why things happen in our lives. All things work together for the greater good and fulfillment of destiny. Walking in my truth has allowed me to discover the freedom to be all that I have been called to be, without apology. I don't question life's moments or the challenges that come with the climb. I recognize that every second, minute and hour of our lives have a purpose.

If no one has ever told you, you can create the life that you want.

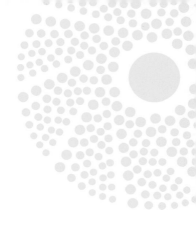

II. STEP OUT

NEVER APOLOGIZE FOR FIGHTING FOR YOURSELF.

—Africa Miranda—

THE FRAMING THOUGHTS

DISCLAIMER: ANYTHING BEYOND this point is reserved for those who are ready to push past average. This book was not written for anyone who is interested in living a life categorized as unexceptional. If you are happy with where you are and feel no sense of urgency to push beyond your current state, pause your reading now. In no way shape or form am I judging you; however, I am suggesting that it might be time to Step Out! The way we decide to live our lives and the pursuits that we choose to embark upon must be our choice and our choice alone. We all want the best for our lives, and this concept takes on different meanings for each of us. Everything written from here on speaks to those who feel a sense of urgency to experience a more abundant life and thrive exponentially. Doing so requires a different level of attentiveness to your surroundings and more importantly, a different set of strategically executed actions toward a desired end. We are preparing to delve into great acts of breaking barriers. Breaking barriers hurts, but do you desire to live above the fray? In doing so, we are thrust into a constant state of testing plans for reaching higher heights in our lives. If we endeavour to go higher, it does not make us magically exempt from pitfalls, trials and tribulations. If anything, making a decision to STEP OUT into unchartered territory dictates that the terrain will be unfamiliar. Taking the initiative to move beyond the regular is not for the faint of heart. Anything that we aspire to is attainable, but mindset is key. No matter how many steps we take, we must be cognisant of our thoughts and intrinsic motivations while remaining in touch with who we are. If you can say to yourself with certainty that you have felt the tugging of purpose and feel compelled to engage and vibrate at the highest levels possible, I say to you, "keep reading."

THE THEORY

STEPPING OUT IS an act of willfully moving into the unknown, because you recognize that what is on the other side is better than the existing. There is "better" for all of us if we are willing to work to bear witness to it. In the realm of possibilities, one who vows to STEP OUT recognizes that there is another layer that can be removed that dares to expose an upgraded version of you. The concept of stepping out is the concerted effort to change the trajectory of our lives with small, yet decisive action. Simply stated, to STEP OUT means to allow the world to be a launching pad for success.

To STEP OUT is to engage in an uphill mountain climb. This part of the process requires you to recognize that the risks require resiliency. This level is designed for you to categorize your attempts to create a better life while making failures a thing of the past. Instead, you must value and regard every moment as a teachable experience. The bumps and bruises of your experiences will serve as reminders for you to pivot and change directions along your path to success. You now know without question that no matter what happens, your commitment to STEP OUT is not a mistake.

It should be noted that the decision to STEP OUT will be met with increased scrutiny. To be the best at whatever you desire to do, also dictates that you not be hard to find. Separating yourself from the crowd, increases your visibility, and you will begin to gain some attention that you might not have previously received. The more visible you become, the more you establish yourself as a target for arrows laced with the opinions of others. Remember, these opinions must be of no concern to you.

THE ANALYSIS

HAVE YOU EVER stopped to ask yourself "Who Cares?" Believe me, it's time well spent. A good friend told me how she would go to her mother when she felt wronged or slighted by others, and her mother would reply "who cares?" She said she learned, as an adult, that her mother's response was not one of disregard for the subject matter, but she was providing a simplistic, yet profound retort that revealed value in living life according to one's own terms. As we would ponder many of life's decisions through our discussions, her mother's expression was a bold reminder that the small things and opinions of others don't matter.

If you took the time to analyze in truth, you'd likely be surprised at the percentage of your life you live to please others. There is a heavy burden associated with people pleasing. As much as we believe that people are concerned about what we are doing and the series of events occurring in our lives, people don't care as much as we convince ourselves that they do. Furthermore, I can assure you that there is a select few who care enough that their opinions should impact how we live and who we decide to become.

For me, the phrase "Who cares" has evolved as an invaluable tool for the discovery of truth. To ascend, the discovery of truth can not be optional. When we recognize our truths, the smoke of public opinion clears, and the path to discover true purpose in our lives is revealed. When we forfeit the opinions of others to discover our truths, we consciously position ourselves to thrive amidst what we are most passionate about, and we discover our purpose.

BELIEVE THERE IS MORE

IF YOU'VE EVER paused and asked yourself if this is it, there is a possibility that you might have been feeling overwhelmed. We can all relish and marvel in the fact that life always has more to offer us. Whatever level of success you hope to achieve, whatever action you feel justified in making towards the realization of a dream will not be actions buried in vanity. In all your work, do recognize that there is more for you. Wherever you are right now, in this moment, are visions that reflect that this is not it. There is more success that awaits you. There is more abundance with your name on it. Affluence, plentitude, opulence are your birthright. Your access has been granted.

THE PERSONAL TESTIMONY

A DIFFICULT PATH DENOTES A HIGHER CALLING.

—Africa Miranda—

LIFE AFTER REALITY TV in 2013 was challenging to navigate. My show, *The New Atlanta,* wasn't renewed for a second season, and I felt like I was suffocating in Atlanta. I was still booking modeling campaigns and commercials and still on the road performing with the corporate band I had been a part of for the last two years. I was a working talent and had a bit of local notoriety. To anyone on the outside, it would seem that all was well, and on the surface it was. I just couldn't ignore the nagging feeling that there was more for me, and I was settling. I toyed with the idea of moving back to New York but was hesitant because I had left the city five years prior feeling very defeated. Unwilling to commit fully to moving, I came to New York for a six week stay in April of 2014 to test the waters. It was the perfect whirlwind romance to suck me back in. I partied, went on dates, had some promising meetings... all signs pointed to this being the right move. I was ready to face the Big Apple once again, and this time I wasn't going to lose. I came back to Atlanta, sold what I could of my furniture, put the rest in storage, and bought a one way ticket to NYC. At this time, I was the face of one of the largest Black hair care brands, and I had a manager and a publicist. I just KNEW this time it would be different.

I was used to being an "it" girl in Atlanta. I was booking commercials and other projects easily, and my face was on billboards and magazine ads. I assumed (a little egotistically) that I would be received the same way upon my grand return. Ah, no. I was treated by most like just "a girl from a reality show." In many spaces, I was politely dismissed. I struggled to find a theatrical and commercial agent. I went from multiple auditions a week to one every few months, and I found those on my own by scouring casting websites. As my bank account dwindled, my depression grew. I wondered if I had made a mistake; turning my life upside down, yet again. What was I in search of? In Atlanta, I was on television, in magazines, had a great creative circle and a little money in my pocket, but I didn't have my own voice.

Up to this point in my career, I was being led by agents, my manager, and people I viewed as more experienced and seasoned in the business. I was happy to listen to any voice other than my own. After my experience on reality tv, I knew I didn't want that to continue. I looked at my "career" and had to really ask myself what I wanted. I was scared to admit that I didn't really know. I thought the show would've lasted, at least, a couple of seasons, and I would have had the time to ride the wave from that into...something. Now I had to figure it out. Back in the city that nearly broke me once before. The fall of 2014 into the spring of 2015 was one of my darkest times. I stopped working with my manager of almost ten years, released the publicist I could no longer afford, and just sat still. During this same time, my hair, which was the main source of my income, was severely damaged by a longtime stylist. As a result, I had to cut off the majority of it off. I also developed allergies that were exacerbated by stress so bad that I had to take asthma medication. Shit was bad! Clearly, the universe was telling me that a total upheaval was necessary.

In March of 2015, something happened to change the course of my life. Periscope was created. This live-streaming app was created to connect global communities and allow people to broadcast their daily life to the web from their phone. I found the app seven days after it was created, and as an early adopter, I quickly grew an online tribe of fellow "Scopers." My viewers were "The Africans." I was immediately drawn to the ease with which I could connect with my audience in real time, and it allowed me to enjoy social media again in a way that I could control. I wasn't prepared for a lot of the ugliness and scary side of social that can come when you're on a television show, and I was really kind of traumatized. In the early days, Periscope was fun, and I enjoyed sharing my life, my way. As the app continued to grow in popularity, I used it as a platform to connect with fellow creatives. It was cathartic to share my stories, and I realized, as I answered questions from people who wanted to further their journey, that I really did have helpful insight to offer. At this same time, I had also thrown myself into "digital grad school." I was taking online courses to learn how to better market myself on social media, and define the ever elusive "personal brand." What I realized in so many of these courses was that as a creative, I already had many of the intangibles. Some of the technical aspects and follow through needed work, but none of these courses was really speaking to my fellow actors, singers and models. I started regular "Talent Scopes" to share tips and strategies with creatives on how to leverage social media for higher visibility and curating their online presence. In one of these scopes "Step Up, Step Out, and Shine" was born. It was born of the idea that as a talent you shouldn't be using the antiquated business model of being "discovered." You, instead, should be using all of the new methods you have at your fingertips to stand out.

Once I gave this practice a name, it became my new religion. I had a clear creative direction, and it became plug and play. Within the next year, I was a Shorty Award finalist for Periscoper of the year, and I gave my first keynote address at the second Periscope Summit. I was invited to speak on panels and at events all over the country. Major brand partnerships followed, and I was acting again. Soon, I was even developing my own luxury beauty company. Even though I didn't quite see it at the time, I believed that there was more for me; I longed for more opportunities in my life. I knew that I couldn't continue putting the responsibility of my success on others; I had to own it. I had to push myself; I had to work harder and challenge myself more than I had done in the past. If I wanted to become the version of myself that I always knew was possible, it was time to STEP OUT. To Step Out means that you recognize that your comfort zone is a place of the past. This is the second key to prosperity and a life filled with freedom.

EIGHT

PROACTIVE VS. REACTIVE

MAKE IT HAPPEN. DON'T LET IT HAPPEN.

—Africa Miranda—

YOU HAVE ONE job, and it is to become the creative director of your own life. While there are elements that were never meant for you to control, you have unprecedented levels of power and decision making stock that force you to ask the question: How bad do I really want it? The term "it" takes on many different meanings for each of us. Recognizing what it is that you are chasing is the first step towards taking the lead to will what you want in your life.

Initiative is the name of the game, and lots of it. At this stage, your ability to think ahead, plot, plan and prosper relies heavily on intentionality. In the absence of intent, we can easily be swayed. Intentional living will make you do the work when you are not up for the challenge or when you simply don't feel like it because you know the end result. Learning to not waste time is critical. Find the thing that you will work unceasingly for and pursue it relentlessly.

Too often, we journey through life, letting things happen to us instead of making things happen. Being proactive is about reclaiming your time to proudly serve as the captain of your fate. Careful management of the factors that you control positions you for the win. Willful living is the ultimate indicator of empowerment. In this space, every thought, every action, every result can be analyzed to determine if we are on the path we so desire.

RECLAIM YOUR POWER

YOU ARE NOT a victim. This statement in no way belittles the things that have happened to you. Every face has a story; there is not one person without peril. The things that have happened in your life were assigned to you because you were also given the power to conquer them. Even when you don't feel strong, there is a presence of unprecedented power that lies within the depths of your soul. Thinking, dreaming and thriving in power are your birthrights. Walking in power is a continuous process. It is up to you to determine where your power increases and the strategies that you must keep in rotation to ensure that you are better, wiser, and stronger with every passing day.

You are capable of doing hard things. You are equipped to command the attention of the resources within your grasp. Forget the belief that some people are born with more power than others. This simply isn't true. Power is activated through execution.

There is also untapped strength in freeing yourself of the need to be liked and accepted by everyone. In some instances, being proactive and making decisions that are best for you won't always result in being liked by others. You can't lose sleep over this. This journey requires layers to be shed and bags to be put down. In my life, I've received the divine gift of friendships at every level of my journey, and these friendships were integral to my growth and survival. Trust and believe the same will be delivered to you.

BE INTENTIONAL

TO TRULY BE proactive means that every effort you exert has meaning and that every step taken is towards the fulfillment of purpose. Deciding what you want to do and then doing it is the embodiment of intentionality. One of the best ways to achieve a desired result is to visualize yourself living in the result, but it must be recognized that none of this happens overnight. There are levels to this.

As a child, it is likely that you played make believe. As an only child, I spent countless hours creating an alternate universe where I acted out everything my heart desired. There was nothing more gratifying than being the figure that you chose to play. Whether alone or in a group, and if only for a brief moment in time, you believed that you were whoever you dreamed of being. This was powerful then, and it is powerful now. Programming your mind to believe that you are the version of yourself that you wish to become allows you to visualize yourself and your reality as you wish for it to unfold. This act sets a power chain of command and energy into motion. You need this type of energy in the atmosphere.

Being present in the moments that happen in your life, also cultivates intentionality. We are inundated with technology and messages from external forces that cloud our ability to be present when life unfolds. Being aware of our surroundings, the people in it and our disposition during given moments, allows us to see the forest from the trees. When we can recognize how moments propel us forward and allow us to feel and be fulfilled, we are empowered to decode the "why" of our experiences. This information proves to be invaluable for the road ahead.

RECLAIM YOUR TIME

IF YOU AREN'T using your time to live with intention, choices for your life and the direction that it takes are being made by default. There are no other options. Life eventually reveals what works and what does not work in your favor. It is up to you to be obedient and present enough to see and hear the signs. When the signs are in clear view, you have the power to make a decision to choose how your time is spent. The key is to alleviate activities that no longer serve your intended purpose. If you recognize that there is something that you want to change about your life, you must take the first step to changing how you spend your time. Listen to Auntie Maxine...Reclaim it.

Consider changing your patterns. It's been stated on several occasions that how you start your day reveals a great deal about how you live your life. It is possible that the way you begin or end your day can make a difference. Do you need to meditate before your day starts to gain clarity? Maybe, you can benefit from working out at the beginning of your day in order to meet your health and fitness goals because like me, your workout capacity diminishes as the day goes on. You can benefit from waking up earlier and spending time reviewing your list of items that you plan on accomplishing that day. We can purchase planners, add calendar dates and reminders to our phones, but the best judge of how your time is spent will be you. After you have determined how your day should begin, consider a pattern for how you desire for it to unfold. Consider building in moments of self-care and breaks. No matter how much we believe that we can produce our work with no breaks, we are not capable of doing so, nor should we. The patterns of how our day is spent reveal all that we need to know about productivity. Ultimately, we must learn to run the day and not allow the day to run us. It doesn't take years to change a pattern; it literally takes a moment.

PUSH THROUGH

WHEN YOU DON'T feel like working, work harder. There is someone who is happier than you are with less than what you have. Someone is being resourceful and proudly creating, building and overcoming obstacles with access to less resources than you have. There is someone who is appreciative of the journey that you could potentially be taking for granted. The phrase "no one cares, work harder," rings true because hard work comes with the territory. This is not to disregard true feelings of anxiety, depression and other mental disorders that require the support of licensed professionals. These types of feelings are important and deserve undivided attention. However, proactivity demands that we move past thoughts of what we don't *feel* like doing at the moment and just doing it now. The work that it takes to vibrate on a higher level will not go away, nor can it be replaced. We must assume responsibility for advancing past anything that can potentially stop or hinder progress.

Observing good mental health practices is important. Your desire to fulfill purpose will require exertion of your emotional energy. This also means that you can expect to experience an increase in attacks that will affect your mental well being. The most startling factor is that many of the attacks that you will face will be from those whom you believed to be your greatest supporters. Your greatest tests will be in your own backyard. What strategies will you have in place to keep you sane when you feel like losing your mind? What moves will you make when friends become foes? What train of thought will you adopt when nothing goes according to plan? How will you react when life throws you a curveball that forces you to revisit past hurt or pain? Make that therapist appointment; I did, and it was a lifesaver. Journal your thoughts. Speak kindly to yourself. You deserve to be where you are, and you must fight to stay there. Although life can throw some unexpected blows, taking responsibility for your well being and doing the work in spite of what is happening around you, will allow the momentum to continue. No matter what comes your way, push through it.

LEVERAGE YOUR LIFE

HOW WILL YOU use what you've got to get what you want? Who do you know that can connect you, teach you, or invest in you? Consider the fact that everyone that you have ever met has a greater purpose in your life. You have not interacted with all of the people that you have come in contact with for no reason. Leveraging your life also means that you recognize the value in leveraging the people in it. Every person, who has ever graced the face of the earth owns gifts and talents. This also means that there are no limits to the skill sets that you can access. Consider building a network of people whose gifts and talents align with your intentions. Out of fear of looking desperate, I was always afraid to reach out to my network and leverage the relationships that I had formed. I also was afraid of rejection, and I felt for a long time that I wasn't worthy of the help or connections they could provide. Who do you know that can connect you, teach you, or invest in you? A few years ago I was sitting with Erika, one of my sorority sisters, and going on and on about my career...my lack of progress, goals that I wanted to achieve but didn't know how and just general "woe is me" conversation. She listened patiently (as she always does) and then asked me if I had asked anyone I knew for help or told anyone in my circles what I wanted to do. I hadn't. She immediately told me to make a list of everyone that I knew and how they could help me. That list was a total game changer. Seeing the names on paper gave me a guide to follow, and one by one I started checking off the people I contacted. Not all panned out, but many did and I'm reaping the benefits of it even today. The universe rewards action and in that moment I became more proactive about my life and career than I had ever been.

Everything that has happened to you, including every experience and every moment in time, has contributed to who you are. Taking the initiative to reflect upon the series of events that compose your life and the lessons gleaned, give you clear indicators for the journey ahead and how you should position yourself in it.

WEED YOUR GARDEN

WHILE YOU SHOULD be connecting with people who can leverage the future you want, you should also be finding ways to separate yourself from those who can't see the value in your quest to evolve. Let's be clear, you can still love people without allowing them to influence your levels of ascension. While we're at it, it should also be noted that it is not your responsibility to heal everyone with whom you come in contact. You owe it to your purpose and your destiny to remain on track.

Taking time to consider who adds wood to your fire is well spent. You must separate yourself from anyone who does not see the potential in you. Everyone around you should add something to your life. Likewise, you should also be speaking life into those around you. If for any reason you find that you are unable to, it is a sign that your presence is not an added benefit to their journey. To attract better, you must remain focused on becoming better. Becoming better also means not resembling the crowd. Discovering what you are passionate about and acting from that passion is a phenomenal way to be impactful. Not only is passion contagious but it is also generated within. It won't be hard to discover those around you who share similar passions and those who don't. This is another way to separate yourself from the crowd.

BE TRANSPARENT

IF YOU SWEAR to tell the truth, the whole truth and nothing but the truth, you will be ushered into a life of abundance with clear expectations and outcomes. Transparency is life! To be transparent, you must first know exactly who you are and how you wish to present to the world. How you want to be identified and known should be crystal clear to everyone. Any confusion present cancels your intentionality. If you want to be the go-to expert for "X," then you should live and breathe "X." It is not enough to simply look the part, you must also do the work to be the most knowledgeable or well versed in your desired lane. This helps people to understand why they need to seek you out when they are in search of "X." It is equally important that who you are behind closed doors aligns with the who you want the world to see. It's hard to be fake, and quite frankly, no one has time for it. It absorbs way too much energy to live in the shadows of who you pretend to be when the real you is dying to be revealed.

The more you learn to master yourself, the more you learn to focus on what is unique and most important to you. Speak up. Keep others informed about what is important to you. To Step Up, Step Out, and Shine means putting yourself out there and being your best advocate. No one should have to guess your goals or turn over rocks to find you. You also have a responsibility to show people who you are, not just tell. Talk is great, but actions are worth their weight in gold. Thanks to social media and the constant documentation of our lives, people are always watching. We must make sure that our behaviour is matching our motives and intentions. Being clear, upfront and transparent will help you to command the attention and respect that you deserve along your journey.

NINE:

AUTHENTICITY, SELF-*ADVOCACY* AND ACCEPTANCE OF OTHERS

YOUR AUTHENTICY CAN'T BE
TRADED FOR APPROVAL.

—Africa Miranda—

HAVE YOU EVER wondered how long it actually takes a person to figure out who they are? It is likely that you can't answer and neither can I. The quest to discover who we are and how we will present ourselves to the world is one of the great challenges of life. We can spend our entire lives discovering who we are. There is immense beauty in this process if we recognize that life is and has always been about the journey, as opposed to the destination. At various points in our lives, there are so many signals that point toward specific finish lines that often trick us into believing that we have to realize certain milestones on specified deadlines to be worthy of life's glory. These messages are so strong that they often lead us into pitfalls of consistent comparison. This can ultimately result in a lack of appreciation for the present and enhance our failure to recognize the opportunities available to us. Taking the time to do the internal work of understanding our motivations, beliefs and what we are passionate about is the only way to remove the layers and get to the core of our authentic selves. Anything less is simply fool's gold. When we are fortunate enough to tap into new levels of authenticity, we must protect it at all costs.

Protecting who we are also means accepting others for who they are. In many instances, this means letting go of the images of who we believe someone to be and how we rely on them at a given juncture in our journey.

MOVE

THE PERSON WHO stands in the way of your next move is not hard to find. Although troublesome to admit, we self-sabotage much of what we are destined to accomplish through negative self-talk, doubt, fear, anxiety, naysayers and other facets that are not meaningful towards fueling the fire of our journey. Until we learn how to move out of our own way, new levels will not be realized. Overthinking everything and holding on to the past smolder the fire, and we are left questioning why we end up with smoke. How many times have you asked for the universe to send you a sign and then ignored it? We are all guilty, but failing to yield or even stop only increases our chances of collision. Sometimes, "moving" means sitting still. Sometimes "moving" can mean gathering your thoughts and crafting a strategic plan before taking flight. We've become obsessed with appearing and actually bragging about being busy, but are we driving in circles? Let your internal GPS be your guide. Can you imagine what could happen if you moved out of your own way?

TAKE CARE

IF YOU DESIRE to reach new levels in your life, you must demand that no person, place or thing come in between you and your dreams. That also means you. We can be so engaged while chasing goals that we skip opportunities to nurture the most important person. You can't pour from an empty cup. Attempting to live up to the expectations that others have for us, compounded with those we have managed to ingrain in our minds for ourselves, can be exhausting. In a twenty-four hour span, we are expected to like, comment and post high quality photos, exercise, make "boss moves", stay connected to friends, "hustle," serve as the liaison for "team no sleep," donate to charity, perform community service, "stay woke," become an overnight vegan AND work. Where is the time allotted for self-care? Have we considered that we also need moments to unplug and rejuvenate? There are times when we can benefit from silencing the noise to hear what our internal messaging is saying. Your mind, although over-stimulated from the chatter of the world, has its own internal structure that is often more in sync with what should be happening and what actions you need to be taking more than you know. Furthermore, the less time we take to listen to and care for ourselves, the less we recognize our voices. Knowing what your mind, body and soul are asking of you is an action that can't be overlooked or negated. Don't let the world distract you from the fact that self-care is important. It isn't just some fluff activity wrapped up in feminine stereotypes. It is absolutely necessary for your survival.

WEAR BLINDERS

COMPARISON IS THE thief of joy. It comes like a thief in the night to reprogram and redirect your thoughts and beliefs about yourself. These pitfalls are placed strategically in your path as tests. If you can't deny the spirit of comparison along your journey, you will never reach your full potential because you are too busy dissecting someone else's progress. If I'm feeling particularly antsy about my life movement I step back from social media for a break. Learn who and what your triggers are. We're human, and I'm not going to sit here and act like I don't feel some way when I don't get certain invitations or opportunities (I'm still on my journey!). To check these feelings, I ask myself three questions: What are my current successes? What am I thankful for? What can I do better? Answering these questions always brings levity. I'm usually doing better than I thought. I have much to be thankful for, and there is always room for me to improve. This allows me to not get caught up in the hit parade online and stay grounded. Always remember that no one person's path to success is the same. Life is not, nor will it ever be, a one size fits all scenario. Don't look around, look within.

DON'T READ THE COMMENTS

WHAT DO THE opinions of others have in common with your opinion of yourself? Nothing! Nowadays, everyone has an opinion and they have a ton of options from which to publicly display them (Too many!). Remaining unbothered in the face of opinions from the masses is beneficial in more ways than one way. I receive so much unsolicited advice from people on what to do with my life and my businesses. My "thank you" with a smile is the equivalent of scrolling through negative comments online. Don't engage. Most people in life and online are just talking because they can. It is almost impossible to change their minds, and all you're doing is frustrating yourself and wasting precious time that could be spent on your own development. If you are driven by what others think, it becomes increasingly harder to make peace with what you believe to be true about who you are. It can also be detrimental to adopt other's perceptions of you because they have not been given the vision for your life. That is reserved for you. This vision comes with the responsibility of seeing it through to fruition. Clouding your judgement won't get you to the promised land. Make peace with what you believe about yourself and strive on a daily basis to fall deeply in love with the reflection staring back at you.

PUT DOWN THE GAVEL

BELIEVE IT OR not, we are all running the same race. Every face that you encounter is fighting a battle that you know nothing about. Serving as the judge and the jury for those around you keeps you occupied and more importantly off task. One of the hardest things I had to admit about myself is that I was very judgy, especially with people close to me. I told myself that

I was judging because I cared, and it was out of love. I'm pretty sure if you asked the people close to me, they would tell you that it didn't feel loving. Learning to allow people to be exactly who they are and taking time to recognize them for who they are can save a great deal of disappointment. There are times when people will not exceed or even meet the expectations that we set for them. It is possible that the bar is too high or that the presence of other circumstances unbeknown to you are blowing in the wind. Acceptance of self also means acceptance of others. Exercising compassion better equips you to exercise compassion towards yourself.

OPEN YOUR MIND

HAVE YOU EVER stopped to think that you've imprisoned yourself with a facade of who you believe you should be? This mindset could be occurring for a myriad of reasons. We've all fallen victim to attempting to become who others want us to be. The image of yourself in your mind, perfectly formed, is simply a mirage. Until we learn to open our minds and get lost in the right direction, we can never evolve into the most profound versions of ourselves. There is something that is so sublime about allowing ourselves to be molded like clay by our experiences and those whom we encounter. In every new moment that we are blessed to bear witness, we are exposed to new opportunities to believe with our imaginations and to consider our possibilities. The greatest lesson that we can glean from life is to recognize that we can become more than our wildest perceptibility. We don't even have the ability to conceive all of the wondrous things that can manifest in our lives. By reprogramming ourselves to believe that there is more and that abundance is for us, we can create a shift in the atmosphere that can prove to be awe inspiring.

LET GO

YOU HAVE THREE options: let go, hold on, or be towed. Our need to control every aspect of life is not far fetched. There are so many elements that we are not in control of, at times we can feel helpless. At times we can feel helpless and out of control. A bird's eye view helps us to understand that letting go is far easier than attempting to hold on to something that was never real, no longer exists, or bears no fruit. There is a pre-established plan in place for each of us that holds our destiny. While this doesn't mean to wander aimlessly about, it does mean that we must take cues from those things that are stagnant and even dead in our lives. Immense power is revealed when we let go of the people, places and things that hold us down. Letting go of old ideas that no longer align with our future goals or evolution, is critical. Denouncing those preconceived notions about who we expect people to be and the roles that we desire for them to serve in our lives can be painful, but letting go can also lead us to prosperity and peace of mind. Here's the real thing, it is absolutely possible to grieve things that are still alive but dead in our lives. Make it a ritual if you need to but whatever you do, stop watering the concrete.

TEN

BUILDING BLOCKS:
BUILDING BRAND YOU

EXECUTE *WITH* EXCELLENCE.

—Africa Miranda—

IN A WORLD where so many wear veils of inauthenticity, those who bear their soul will win.

There are several ways to communicate who you are, what you do and your intended message to the masses. The win is embedded in our ability to take responsibility for our success. Factors regarding success in our own lives should not and must not be left up to others. We must discover the confidence and optimism to face our fears and take the leap towards the life of abundance of which we dream. Having a positive impact or helping solve problems for others is the equity that we need in order to build a substantial brand. The commitment to serving as lifelong learners and communicating our messages to the world are the pieces to the puzzle that must be addressed.

SAY WHAT?

WHY DO WE spend so much time trying to figure out what message we want the world to know about us? In part, it could be because we can easily draw a parallel between our message and our purpose. The two are indeed connected at the seams. Whether intentional or not, we are sending and receiving messages on a daily basis about who we are and our belief systems that drive other people's perceptions of us. The unspoken acts, such as the way in which we live our lives, is our message. Everything that we do, say, and the way that we exist in the world speak more profoundly than any set of carefully crafted words or phrases that we can concoct. Preparing to achieve new levels means that we take the time to analyze, strategically tailor, and account for the evolution of our intended messaging. What we say determines how we will be received by our intended audiences.

The first step, after recognizing that we want more and that we have more to say, is analysis. Taking time to carefully assess what we are saying and determining if it mirrors who we want the world to see is as powerful as it gets. You are speaking, even if you don't recognize that you are. Your daily conversations, text messages, social media engagement, and person to person inter-actions are all up for discussion. What are the patterns and trends regarding what you are saying? The proof is in the content that you produce. As you begin to take note of the content that you are producing, the next step is to analyze it to determine if it is indeed relaying your intended messaging. Do you want to be known as a thought leader in a particular arena or an influencer in the digital space? Maybe, you want to be an expert on a particular topic or in a specific profession. If this is true, your output should reflect who you want the world to see. If you realize that your words and actions aren't lining up, you have the power to adjust and fix them. It's your message, so own it!

Not only must we determine what we want to say and how we want to say it, but we must also find a way to account for evolution. Ten years from now, you will not be the same person that you are today. If you are, it is time to stop and reassess because stagnation is crippling. Your new normal is that you must get comfortable with constant growth. The truth is that it hurts like hell. The constant stretching and pulling are not for the faint of heart. To actualize the best version of yourself, you can't remain the same. Amidst the change of who you are, will also come the change in the delivery of your message, even if your core intent is the same. With every passing moment, we must strive to be better, wiser and stronger.

RAISE YOUR VIBRATIONS?

YOUR ABILITY TO vibrate at higher frequencies sets the tone for your brand and its associated value. Vibrations are a real thing. Until you get to a point in your life where you consistently humble yourself to them, there will always be a lot left to be desired regarding your tribe. Ignoring the energy that is produced in the presence of the people that you encounter is a missed opportunity for greatness. Vibrations are indicators to our hearts and souls that lead us to the answers that we so seek about everything. Trusting your instincts explicitly means knowing the truth about people. When I was a small child, I felt things very deeply and was very affected by the energy of others. As I got older, I ignored my intuition and the messages being sent to me because it scared me, and I wasn't ready to listen. Now, that I am in tune and have learned to listen, I can usually tell within moments what someone's intentions are and if my interaction with them will be positive. Learning to trust connections and even when to break them is a muscle that will develop. While some would argue that we should not journey through life using our heart as a guide, there is great wisdom buried within us. Whether or not you choose to listen to your "soul speak" further indicates your levels of growth and preparedness for ascension. The intentional recognition of energy is an intricate part of this process.

STOP CHANGING THE PRICE

THE SELF-WORTH STRUGGLE is real, but it ends here. Stop struggling with your worthiness. Your next level requires the version of you who does not question the value of self. You are preparing to fry big fish., and you know your way around the kitchen. You don't need any comparison for how you do what you do when you do it. No one can be you better than you. You have arrived at a point in life where you look in the mirror and find yourself saying "Yasssss" because you've managed to give yourself so many compliments. There is no harm in owning your worth (*and adding tax*). For much of my career, I trusted others to negotiate for me and set my price for my services. Once I took the reins, I was hesitant to give my rate when asked, for fear of missing out on the opportunity. I realized I was never going to get what I was truly worth until I believed it and was able to unapologetically put a number on it. If you were asked your rate for a dream project and money was no object, what would it be? Start there. Figure out the least amount of pay you can accept that will cover your time and expenses and don't go below that number. Whatever you're charging right now as you read this, raise it. Those that value your work will pay. What you'll find is that by setting this new tone, positive financial energy will come your way, and it will grow exponentially.

Remember that you will not be qualified every time you are called, but that's not an excuse to not pick up the phone. To get to next level and witness your best life ever, you've got to let go of the need to be completely ready. There will never be a perfect time for anything to manifest. Allow the universe to thrust you into the opportunities and rise to meet the challenge. You have the ability to do challenging things. Because of your ability, you can step into spaces that you never even knew possible! Moments of greatness occur when you push boundaries and dare to dance with discomfort. When you become sure of the fact that you can count on yourself, you will have no need to discount what it is that you do. Don't adjust your pricing, adjust your expectations of you, and win!

NO FRAUDS

MASKS ARE DANGEROUS. They often obstruct the vision of the wearer and blur the image and perception for the onlooker. Do curate the message of your brand and overall image, but please, be authentic. While we recognize that perception is everything, the truth trumps all. Remaining legitimate in a world that seemingly embraces fake personas and attributes is not always easy, but there are no limits to the ways in which we can establish ourselves and our brands. The first step towards establishing who you are is acceptance. The foundation of self-acceptance is love. If you don't love the real you, then making this request of others is a moot point. When my hair was damaged, and I was forced to cut it off, I was forced to confront my true feelings on beauty. I was preaching #Team-Natural and telling women all over the world to love themselves as is, and I was only loving myself about seventy-five percent at that point. Confronting these issues and sharing the truth with my audience created a deeper connection with them and also started me on the path that led me here. Everything, including the authenticity of your brand, begins with your ability to decode your strengths and weaknesses and discover love amongst them all. The exercise of gratitude is extremely powerful in this space. What do you appreciate about yourself? What can you count on yourself for? What is unique about you? How can you make the lives of others better? Self-acceptance and self-love go hand in hand, and you are most powerful when you exercise both. Making these attributes a priority is half the battle, when on a mission to realizing authenticity.

Another consideration when establishing your brand in an authentic way is the uniqueness of your journey. You have experienced life in ways that no one else in the world has. Your lens reveals a different story that could have only been captured by you. As the author, you have a responsibility to share that story through your brand. Your story establishes the foundation from which to build a solid brand and reputation. Your story makes you the expert on your experiences. This is the beauty of constructing your brand from your perspective to share with the world. You were given a set of circumstances and a journey because you could handle it. The greater question becomes: How will you leverage all that you have learned, along the way, and the things that you have triumphed, to speak to the world? Your authentic brand is the essence of your soul, your story, your experiences and your expertise. When you consider all of that content, what do you really have to say?

DO THE WORK

THE LIFE YOU lead and the brand that you build are an ever evolving portfolio from which to display your talents and further show why you should be highly sought after in what it is that you have decided to do. With every new layer that you reveal, you should also have work to show for it. When you become explicitly known for what it is that you do, your brand is speaking loudly and clearly to the world. It is what will open doors, put you on planes, in front of crowds, and put money in your pocket.

Excellence is not what we do on occasion; it is what we do repeatedly.

Set standards for the work that is released on your behalf or that bears the name of your brand. The words that you speak and the moments that you spend with others should all be done in excellence. Whether you are building a company, serving as a brand ambassador, or representing any profession, people will never forget the way that you made them feel. With every interaction you have, you can and should leverage relationships to climb and reach higher heights. Ambitious interactions should not be mistaken as selfish intentions. Not only should you be better for the interactions that you are a part of with others, but they should also be better for having interacted with you. New friends can and should represent new opportunities to do what you do best and add to your repertoire. The more opportunities that come your way, the more selective you can be about what you choose to do and the work you add to your list of accomplishments. No matter how good you proclaim to be, your work is the indicator that tells the truest story of what you have been doing along your journey.

BUILD A TRIBE

AS MUCH AS we would all like to believe that we can be great on our own, nothing monumental is accomplished in isolation. You are going places, and you are going to need some help. Taking the initiative to strategically construct a network of people who can do things that you cannot is crucial. There is nothing worse than being filled with potential and faltering because you have more opportunity than capacity to see it through. This was me for so long! Furthermore, there is not enough time, nor is it a good use of resources to attempt to be a master of everything. I spent so many years having moderate success because I was trying to do EVERYTHING. I did a few things well; most things I did moderately, and I had only a few flashes of excellence. I spent more time building myself and not a team, and when I faltered, I had no one to lean on for support.

Take a moment to close your eyes and envision the face of someone with whom you spend a great deal of time. Now, consider what happens to your energy around that person? Does it increase? Do you feel motivated and inspired when you are together? If the answer is "no," consider how big of an impact the person, whom you envisioned, has in your tribe. You are the sum of the people with whom you spend the most time. You can't be the sole motivator in your crew. I am not saying that you can only hang with a tribe of winners, but I am saying that everyone needs to be moving forward with the capability of supporting each other. If you're looked to as the one to motivate the entire circle, it's time to find a new circle.

Do also consider that we miss unexpected blessings because they don't come wrapped in familiar packaging. This is true of people too. Remember the intuition we talked about? This is where you need to flex that muscle. Ask yourself the following: Who pours into you? Who is too busy chasing goals to notice what others are doing? Who talks more about ideas than people? Like all relationships, your tribe should evolve over time. We will have our seasons, and some relationships will remain, while others may fall by the wayside.

GO PUBLIC

IF YOU DON'T shout your brand's message from the rooftops, then who will? Social media has empowered us in ways unimaginable to connect, inspire and authentically engage. It is a must that you discover your niche and strategically execute the art of self-promotion. Let's be clear, creating a brand that you believe the world will covet is simply not enough.

Let's face it, private, social media accounts are for those that wish to fly under the radar. It's called *social* media for a good reason. These platforms were established to allow engagement that knows no boundaries, and they can work in your favor in so many ways, if you open the floodgates. Managing an account on a digital platform that no one can see or interact with is no different than putting on a gold, sequined dress to attend a Friday night football game and being confused as to why people notice you. If your goal is to not be seen, why are you there? Social media is for the purpose of connecting. To maximize the benefit, you've got to do more than just get your feet wet. To put your brand on display and promote it as you should, you've got to dive in.

To be considered *social* on social media, you must find ways to engage. Talk back to the people that talk to you. Answer your DM's, and most importantly, be kind. Keep the same energy that you would want to exchange in person. Do connect with like- minded people whose posts make you say *YESSSS!* You'd be surprised how many people you can discover synergy with in the ever evolving *internet streets*. As you share your message, track the results. Who's saying *YESSSS* to you? Who comments consistently? What are they in search of? Do you have the solution? Your brand should speak to those who are paying attention, and the message should be crystal clear. How can you affect their lives in a positive way? How can what you do, who you are or what you sell solve their problem? Give something. Promote something. Move the people to action. With social media, the microphone is in your hand, speak up!

ELEVEN:

NEW MERCIES: RITUALS FOR DAILY RESTORATION AND RESILIENCE

BE KIND TO ALL. BUT MOST OF
ALL BE KIND TO YOURSELF.

—Africa Miranda—

NO MATTER HOW amazing your life is, there will be days that remind you that you need to reset. There will be times that you will need to feel grace and mercy from the universe and moments in which you seek to be restored. Life is a series of highs and lows, and traveling along the path to greatness means that you are not exempt from the days that prove to be more challenging than rewarding.

The difference between those who weather the storm and those who get left out in the rain is an emergency survival plan. In case of an emergency, such as a failure, emotional distress, rejection, stress, anxiety, and any other force that can have the power to cause harm to our purpose, what is your plan? Whom do you call? What action do you take? What do you read? What song do you listen to? How do you address yourself? Who do you need to stay away from? You need answers. You need a plan of action for these concerns before you have to put it into motion. Approaching life with no plan in place to restore and exercise resilience in the wake of challenges, is a plan to falter. We are indeed strong but need ways to renew our strength on a continual basis. If you are not establishing rituals to restore, then you are establishing a trend of self-sabotage. Sabotage of self does not exemplify strength; your strength is in your ability to plan, predict and prosper amidst moments of peril.

True self-care must be considered from the perspective of mind, body, and soul. It is within these three facets that our true power rests, rules and abides.

MEDITATE

YOUR ABILITY TO reset and refocus will prove to be one of your most powerful tools. Many fail to realize that for optimal performance, the process of clearing your cache is a continuous process. It is not a one and done. Life happens all around us, and it is not hard to be pulled away from your intended course. Recognizing this to be a truth and crafting several outlets that cater to your need to redirect is critical. It is imperative that you consistently evaluate your intended direction and if your current progression will lead you there.

One effective way to determine if you are headed in the right direction is to engage in the act of decluttering your thoughts. Finding ways to alleviate the massive amounts of information that can often get trapped inside of your head is not only a way to relieve undue stress but also to discover your hidden truths. Another way to see what you are truly made of is to rest.

Meditation can improve your quality of rest. Imagine what can happen if you actually wake up feeling refreshed and ready to take on the day! Feeling well rested and recharged can prove to be the relief from anxiety that you never even knew that you needed.

Don't allow social media to trick you into believing that you actually win points by being the captain of #team-nosleep. This is the real fake news and alternative facts. It takes time to develop a meditation practice, so don't get discouraged if you spend most of your first sessions with your mind replaying the last episode of *Insecure*. Eventually, you will settle in and your body will learn to accept the quiet. While you may never be perfect at it (I am definitely still working on my practice), you will be able to reap the benefits of taking a moment to center yourself. Operating from a refreshed state allows us to reap the benefits of living life more intentionally. Intentionality is the only true pipeline to purpose. We must envision ourselves victorious and amidst perfect peace. This is the truest definition of happiness. In the end, that's what we are all after.

COUNT EVERY WIN

SMALL VICTORIES ARE worth counting. Failure to notice what you are achieving incrementally, leaves air and opportunity to count what feels like losses. Overanalyzing moments that resulted in things not going according to plan can be harmful to your ability to bounce back or to strategize. Your ability to classify your small wins is also an indicator of how well you can switch gears to meet the demanding needs of your goals.

Whether big or small, your wins keep you from having a breakdown and keep your self-esteem intact. If you allow yourself to feel like you have not had success of any kind, your perception of self-worth diminishes. I spent so much time chasing large accomplishments that I missed out on enjoying my small moments of progress. I would feel so defeated because I hadn't scaled yet another large mountain (of my choosing), that I failed to realize that I was slowly checking off many items on my childhood wish list. I've always wanted to travel the world as a successful singer. I've performed in Africa, the Middle East and much of the United States, but because I did it as part of a corporate band, it was somehow less than. How many of our deferred dreams have actually been realized, but we haven't noticed because they don't look like the picture in our minds? Why is it that we have an ability to easily recognize what didn't go well, but we struggle to comprehend what did? It is possible that we are wired to see the glass as half empty. Growth is recognizing the glass as half full. Doing so is an invaluable opportunity to identify what's left of a goal to achieve. Adjusting that thinking and recognizing that you do have wins each and every day, can change the trajectory of your ability to achieve. As they say: "perspective is everything." At the end of the day, you should feel good because you have taken action. You should feel good because you are alive. You should feel good because you've decided not to give up. Making a concerted effort to count your wins is synonymous with counting your blessings. The end result is an enjoyable and well deserved finish line.

LET YOUR LIPS SPEAK LIFE

THE WHISPERS INSIDE your head are far more powerful than the words you speak out loudly. Your thoughts are the unfiltered sentiments of your heart. The words that are birthed from your innermost thoughts dictate who you will become and the levels of achievement that you will realize. Your words can be the secret weapon to conquering fears, denouncing doubt and silencing naysayers that smother dreams.

Speaking positively is only half the battle. Embarking upon a journey to become the best version of yourself, also means arming yourself with tools to engage in the powerful act of self-reassurance on a daily basis. Affirming words and your engagement with them must become a part of a continuous ritual for repeated results. It is so important that we know how to build ourselves up with words spoken internally and that we not become reliant on any other source of reinforcement. The tricky part about outside validation is that it does not provide consistency and is often unpredictable. There are too many factors left to chance when we seek the endorsement of others. Doing so can lead to disappointment that is avoidable if we learn to seek authentication from inside. At the end of the day, it is imperative that you always believe that you can count on yourself.

There is also a tremendous amount of trust building that must be established between the reflection you see in the mirror and your heart. Your ability to reinforce yourself is rooted in how confident you are that you will do what you say you will do and that you will achieve the way that you dare to dream. An integral part of building trust during the establishment of an ongoing positive self-talk ritual, is doing the work to eliminate negative self-talk. If someone spoke to us the way that we tend to speak to ourselves, the least of what would happen is that we wouldn't have them in our lives. Yet, every day, we are in a dysfunctional relationship with ourselves. We can post all of the inspirational quotes and memes in the world, but it is all hollow if we aren't being kind to ourselves.

Sometimes, we speak power into things that don't deserve our time or energy. Our mind often allows us to magnify events that transpire in ways that never even come to fruition. Worry, doubt and uncertainty manifest into fear, causing a chain reaction that only succeeds in delaying us or taking us off course. Much of what happens on a day to day basis is miniscule in comparison to the bigger picture. We could all benefit from resisting the urge to blow things out of proportion. Everything that we experience has the potential to benefit our greater good, if we choose to depict it as such. I had to examine the words I used to describe myself and things that happened to me. I had gotten used to the narrative that my life always had some kind of "drama." I would jokingly say that I was "a mess." It may seem lighthearted, but words hold weight, and they manifest. The magnitude and intensity at which you describe what happens and the thoughts that you bring forward can make all the difference in the world. Let your lips speak life.

UNPLUG

TECHNOLOGY, TELEPHONES, AND electronic devices are not just a part of what we do but also who we are. Although we use our devices to organize our lives, track data, remain in touch and be entertained, the consistent flow of outside information can inundate us in ways unimaginable. Whether forcing us to engage in comparison of our lives to the lives of others, or placing a never ending *to do* list at the forefront of our minds, we need a break from the monotony of it all to fully center.

Taking time away from the phone that has now seamlessly become an attachment to our bodies is crucial.

From notifications to checking to see who's liking and commenting on our photos and posts, we can, at times, become overwhelmed as we store messaging that we are not even aware of. In an effort to reclaim my time, I've turned off my notifications. You can honestly do without them. When you truly analyze the question of whether or not there is more value in being notified for every *email*, *like* or *follow*, or maintaining your peace of mind, there is no competition. Even if you are using your social media or your tech for business, your contact information is likely listed. You are able to be reached, and if someone wants or needs to find you, they can.

Making a decision to be accessible on your own terms, places you in the driver's seat. Over exposure can mean finding yourself pulled away from intended tasks, overexertion of your output of energy and over commitment. None of these factors helps you to become the best version of yourself, live your best life or maintain a healthy balance. Your balance will become the by product of your ability to ration your accessibility to outside information and requests. Teaching others what they can expect from you can prove to be a positive strategy for ensuring that there is time to unplug. Strategies, such as an autoresponder to emails, that state that requests will be answered in twenty four or forty eight hours can save you time and energy. Real life goals can be reached when we discover balance in the ability to communicate with others and to unplug in ways that don't affect productivity. You have one life, and more time must be spent living than being held captive by the requests and opinions of others. This is not selfish, it is survival.

SAY HELLO TO YOUR EMOTIONS

IF THE TRUTH is told, feelings and emotions are quite the controversy. On one hand, we are told to trust our feelings and instincts, and on the other hand, we are sometimes hurt by the moments that we allow our hearts to lead. Why do we question our feelings? What makes them wrong or right and who becomes the judge and jury with the final say? The good news is that all power belongs to you. Having a grasp on your emotions and becoming powerful enough to experience the fullness of your feelings, without allowing them to control your actions, form what would be considered real life goals. Just because we feel something, does not mean that we are not to consult our logic. Our feelings are similar to money in our bank accounts; presence does not necessitate purchases. Everyone is afraid of being hurt, but this same hurt that we so desperately avoid is what makes us deny ourselves the option to feel. Life is about feeling and understanding how our feelings and thoughts are intertwined.

Contrary to anything that you have heard, read or believed up to this point, what you feel is real. We have all been gifted with an internal compass that is purposed for both protection and vulnerability. The contrast between the two is so great that we find ourselves in a state of confusion. Our feelings that help us to recognize the good in a situation or people that we encounter is vital. Happiness, excitement, love, joy, and peace are all a part of the divine plan. A person who has never felt the rush of new love, cried or even lost your breath while laughing, is not truly living. Breathing in the fullness of the most gratifying moments of our lives is a necessary step towards true euphoria. We must allow ourselves to feel because not doing so is detrimental in more ways than we can imagine.

Thanks to how performative our culture has become (and a certain rapper), if you're dream chasing or really out here doing it, then you never get tired. I may be alone in thinking this, but it's dangerous. It leads so many to deny feelings of physical and mental exhaustion because they don't want to appear weak or like they don't really "want it." We must learn to recognize our internal cues when they are speaking to us. It is okay to feel tired and exhausted. Not acknowledging the need to reset or refresh can lead to burnout, illness and breakdowns that can require medical intervention. In the most extreme cases, the need to reset has even led people to contemplate or commit suicide. We must stop work shaming others and ourselves. There will be days when you are not feeling it or that you are in your feelings. It's ok. Those moments allow you to exhaust. If you don't acknowledge those feelings, you can set yourself up for rapid destruction.

We must learn to feel the good, the bad and the ugly. Know that while they are valid, your feelings are not permanent. You have the power to change them as you see fit. Your heart, your feelings.

ASK FOR HELP

NOTHING MONUMENTAL CAN be achieved in isolation. A force exists that is greater than each of us. When we connect and exert effort together towards a desired end, we are plugged into a surge of unprecedented power. We must learn to recognize that life is not accidental, and our ability to recognize and make good use of the resources, gifts and talents that exist amongst us can be the difference between the manifestation of our greatest potential and remaining mediocre. We don't accomplish more in isolation. As a matter of fact, we accomplish less when we work alone. Building a team for personal and professional support is key. Working with others is necessary to accomplish your goals and thrive in everyday life. Togetherness can be the evolution of new acquaintances and the alleviation of stress that arises when we work by ourselves.

Those who know how to ask for support in areas that they either don't enjoy or are not naturally gifted in reap tremendous benefits. Have you ever stopped to consider that there are more ways of doing things than the method that you have carved out in your mind? The beauty of soliciting the assistance of others before becoming overwhelmed is that you save yourself from destruction. We are all guilty of taking on too much, and even with our best intentions, we were never created to do or be everything. We've fallen for the lie that asking for help somehow resembles weakness. Nothing could be farther from the truth. We must get help in every area where there is a need. We can benefit from the execution of multi-tasking and the inclusion of other team players.When we consider our self-care and the daily grind that must be initiated to walk in purpose and power, we must conclude that we can't do it alone. Recognizing that you need help is only half the battle, but being brave enough to ask for a hand is a true sign of victory. In asking for help, the key is walking in truth towards the vision that was given to you for your life.

THE INNER CHILD AND SELF-WORK

IF HEALING THE inner child is the first step towards restoration, then assuming responsibility for parenting that same inner child is the second. Our inner child speaks to us and demands to be fed, clothed and entertained. The fabric of who we are has been formed by our positive and negative experiences. Everything that we think, do and say is rooted in the motivations of the inner child. Our ability to restore hope and to prove ourselves resilient in the face of adversity begins with the child within.

Although we are not responsible for what has happened in our childhood, we can resolve that the power to make decisions about our adult lives rests in our hands. Owning the power of our choices is a beautiful thing. Taking steps to heal and restore from past hurts or traumas mean that we understand that we cannot allow our problems to define who we are or who we will become. If there are behaviors, ideals or patterns of thought that are not aligned with where we aspire to go, we must be willing to accept the challenge to do the work to rid ourselves of all signs of toxicity.

There are no limits to how we can do the work to heal the inner child. One step that we can take is to recognize the patterns between the decisions that we make. Are there any correlations between our subconscious? This information is deep below the surface, and some never make the decision to travel there. However, to get something that you have never gotten, you must do something that you have never done. An understanding of this magnitude can lead to new levels of cognition and awareness.

On the path to healing, a guide can be helpful. I had to admit that much of the dysfunction in my life was from my own making. I was also starting to see myself repeating family patterns, and I wanted to break those chains. About five years ago, I tried therapy for the first time. The therapist was a nice, older, white man who was probably very good at what he does, but I didn't feel a connection with him. I didn't feel like he really understood my lifestyle. I am not saying that your therapist has to be from the same race and of the same gender as you, but I do think it is important to feel a level of connection and understanding on a human level. I didn't feel it in that room. Within the last year, I've gone back to therapy, and it has changed my life. For the first time, I feel that I am in control of my emotions and not hurtling through life on an emotional "teeter totter." It is also important to note that you have to be ready. Stepping Out requires vulnerability, fearlessness and a true understanding of self. I am at a point in my life where ascension is the only option, and I am willing to do all of the work required to manifest it. And if you're wondering, yes my therapist is a Black woman.

TWELVE:

NO RESERVATIONS: ADJUSTING YOUR PLANS AND EXERCISING FLEXIBILITY

TRANSFORMATION REQUIRES FLEXIBILITY.
BE OPEN AND TRUST THE CHANGES.

—Africa Miranda—

WHAT IF LIFE went exactly as we planned? Would we be better, wiser or farther ahead? In life, there are no guarantees, but we know that it does not go according to our plans at all times. Believing that we can control the way that life will unfold is reckless. What we do have control over is how we respond. Our ability to make adjustments to our plans is directly linked to what we can achieve, as well as how well we will weather the uncertain moments.

Transformation is a process and a progressive change that fosters awareness and use of inner strength. It will be challenging, but flexibility is the only way to deal with a world that so often changes around us. In those moments, our ability to be stretched and pulled apart and reassembled is where powerful transformation and true growth happen.

CLOSE YOUR EYES

THERE ARE FACTORS and circumstances that affect the way in which you experience life. Some can be witnessed in plain view. The persons with whom we choose to share time and exchange energy, the places that we choose to frequent and the behaviors that we choose to portray, are all factors that we can control. Next level thinking requires us to stop and consider that there are factors and forces, in our lives, that we will never control. There are also energy shifts happening all around us that we can't so easily see. This is even more reason why we must exert less energy towards controlling things outside our scope or reach. You can spend time wondering why things are not going according to your best laid plans, or you can spend time devising a plan that accounts for the need for flexibility and adaptation to life as it happens. Which do you believe will have the best results?

It is hard to know if we are making progress in the right direction with every passing day. In these moments, we must allow our hearts to lead the way. If the action that you are taking does not resonate within you, you may consider closing your eyes to reflect and gain some clarity. Ask yourself some serious questions: What sets my heart on fire? What am I most passionate about? What is the thing that I could talk about for hours? What wakes me up in the middle of the night? What holds my attention? What would I do for free because I love it that much?

There are two types of people in the world—those who feel a sense of happiness and fulfillment from the goals that they achieve and those who are fulfilled from the process of repeatedly setting and achieving goals. Which more accurately defines you? Knowing how you are wired can be the difference when exercising flexibility. There are times when you will need to realign the goal or the destination. Ultimately the true key to happiness is the freedom to do the things that you are most passionate about and those that make the world a better place. Learn to close your eyes to messaging that tells you that you have to do things a certain way. Your path will not be the same as any other person on the planet. Your purpose, your path and your profit have all been constructed just for you.

CHECK REJECTION AT THE DOOR

EMBRACING REJECTION AS an unavoidable part of life expands the realm of possibilities in our lives. Our true flexibility is determined by how well we deal with rejection. If you allow it to serve as a dream killer, the journey towards your greatest achievement is an uphill climb. We benefit, greatly, from considering rejection as a bonafide source of redirection from the universe. As much as it hurts, how could a *direct message* from the universe ever be wrong? In addition to accepting rejection, it is also dually important that we become well versed on how to reject. There is power in rejecting things that no longer serve us or feed our souls. Survival is required in business and in our personal lives, and we must have the ability to break down layers, and add walls in places where we need protection. Anything that stands in our way or that can be categorized as an obstacle serves as a distractor from our intended destination, and it should not be welcomed. When we exercise rejection it doesn't have to be callous. We can learn to reject with care. It is possible to love a person from afar or in a different capacity than what was initially established. If a relationship is not healthy after exerted levels of effort, it can become a factor that stands in your way.

DEAL WITH DISAPPOINTMENT

IN LIFE, YOU will be disappointed more times than you can count. None of us will be exempt from defeat, setbacks, discouragement, error, or miscalculation. Disappointment is ever present, and it can be revealed when dealing with people who appear to come up short in comparison to our expectations or in managing the never ending events that shape who we become.

People won't react to life the same way that you would, because they were not raised the same way that you were. We all come to the table with a plethora of expectations, viewpoints and definitions of how life should be experienced. Setting expectations for others is one of the most prolific ways that we hinder our progress. Instead, we must continue to develop our responses to each occurrence and set realistic goals for what we want to accomplish for ourselves and with others. Spending too much time managing our expectations for others is far less effective than managing our expectations for ourselves. This is not to say that we don't hold people accountable to high standards, but it does mean that when they fall short, we are not so let down that it impedes our progress. We must not get sidetracked by people who are not on track themselves. In those moments, they are of no value to our journey, and we are of no value to theirs. Claiming greatness does not allow for wasted time, energy or experiences. Every moment, even those that disappoint, is another opportunity for us to learn, grow and be cultivated.

PAY YOUR RENT

REALITY CHECKS ARE necessary when making a transformation. It does not matter how amazing you are, no one owes you anything. No miraculous results can be expected simply because we show up. A harvest will not be produced in the absence of the planting of crops. To reap the benefits of the fruits we so desire, we must labor. We also must investigate our true motivations. So much of my life was spent in the pursuit of stardom and what I thought that meant. My greatest successes occurred once my perspective shifted. My focus is now on how I can use my gifts to pour into others. The greatest strides of our lives are made amidst the purpose that we discover in being of service to others. Doing what it takes to make the world a better place is not optional; it is what we are called to do. When we act less from motives rooted in selfish patterns of thought, we invest more in answering a higher calling. It is in this space that real life occurs, and in these moments, we create pathways for others and inspire hope. These times help us to forget about the woes of life, and they enhance our ability to get lost in purpose. Offering our gifts and talents is the rent that we pay for taking up space in the world. On a daily basis, we are called to build a life that accommodates intentional giving. Personal convenience should not take precedent in our calling to serve. Living life in this manner requires us to ask ourselves some challenging questions that lead to answers that should change the way we see ourselves in the world.

HOW CAN I be better?

With every passing day, our goal must not be perfection but evolution towards the absolute best versions of ourselves. Maintaining a vision of who we desire to be at the forefront of our minds is critical. Even on the days that we don't feel like being who we aspire to be, we must learn to adopt patterns of acting, and thinking that are conducive towards growth. We must also learn to admit that evolution is not always comfortable, but it is the only viable way to walk in our greatest power. Growth can not be realized until the process of removing layers has been initiated.

HOW CAN I be impactful?

Have you ever stopped to think that you are the solution? Someone in the world has a problem that you have the capability to solve through your presence, the information that you possess, or a skill set that you have mastered. The world needs you now more than ever. Recognizing that you are a solution to a problem that needs solving allows you to dig deeper to tap into your power, passion and purpose. Purpose is waking up in the morning and pondering how you can make a difference in the life of others. This practice, morphed into daily life, sets you apart from so many. It's no secret that life's many hardships and obstacles often seem insurmountable, and many wake up and only consider problems. Gamechangers, innovators and trendsetters wake up and initiate the process of solutions. The next level of you requires you to be different. The next level of you requires you to lead the charge to become acclaimed for the solution that you can offer the world.

THROW THE WHOLE MEASURING CUP AWAY

IF THE TERM "fair" is still a part of your vocabulary, consider removing it. What is the basis for how we categorize what is fair? How can we compare life, circumstances, the allocation of resources, or offerings of success from one person to another? No dynamic or perspective is the same. Our experiences, intrinsic motivations, and the way in which our lives unfold are as vast as the wind. It's likely that our first engage-ment with the term fair was during our childhood. We were programmed to whine and throw tantrums when things did not appear to be equal amongst peers. This strategy wasn't productive then and it isn't now.

The more time we spend recognizing what we believe to be imbalances in the scales of life, the more energy we devote to how unfair we believe life to be. Time is the one resource that we can not retrieve; it must not be wasted by any means. Instead of focus-ing on what we believe to be unfair, we can reap more benefits from finding ways level the playing field. No one has the power to tip the scale of favor in your life the way that you do. You must believe this with your whole heart and every fiber of your being. What you believe allows the universe to conspire with you to con-ceive it in reality. There is vast power in your thoughts and what you can imagine. We were all born into the world with a variety of negative and positive circum-stances, but how we choose to allow those factors to control our decision making in our choices of people, relationships and investments will make all the differ-ence for how the story ends.

If there is any aspect of your life that you do not like, change it. If there is any aspect of someone else's life that you find desirable, admire it and create your own version.. It is not possible for you to have someone else's life, nor should you desire it. We have no idea what a person has experienced privately to live the life that we see publicly. Make no comparison but do take action towards leveling up to become the person that you desire to become.

ALLEVIATE OBSESSION

IT IS LIKELY that you have made a detailed plan of how you wish for life to unfold, what you will accomplish, and who should be present during the various stages of your experiences. There is nothing wrong with vision; it is the key to remaining true to the goals that we set in motion. The problem with the picture that you visualize is that you can't see the divine vision that is far greater. Often, the divine vision, that is the true drive for our existence and being, does not always mirror what we see. What we don't often realize is that we have the power to add momentum or impede progress along the way. Remaining fixated on achieving a goal a specific way does not allow us to benefit from the value of the doors that life will open. Instead, we can view new courses of action and directions as obstacles. Every factor that changes your plan is not harmful to your ability to arrive at your final destination. If we stop to realize that the journey, the destiny, and the outcome are not factors that we have complete control over, we can also find peace in the fact that life has more to offer than what we can conceive. It is not possible to guarantee specific outcomes for specific actions, but that should not detour us in any way. We are most powerful when we serve as co-pilots, assisting and receiving direction from our purpose. Relinquishing control and allowing divine purpose to serve as an internal GPS, opens the realm of possibilities.

PIVOT

IF YOU ARE not experiencing passion that wakes you up in the morning, a pivot can be just the power move that you've long awaited. Abundant life is inclusive of passion and purpose that fuels your dreams and leads you to discover your greatest transformational power. You must know that every road will not take you to your final, desired destination. While we recognize that we can't control every aspect of the journey, knowing when to change the course is key. The old ways won't open new doors. A change of course, the execution of a new idea, an exploration of new scenery, or engagement with new associates, can all prompt a shift in the course of events that unfolds in your life. It can be dangerous to ride a dream until the wheels fall off. When we recognize that life is not going as we had intended or that we are not making continuous progress, a pivot is necessary. This doesn't mean that you are closing the door on something you love forever, it just may be time to reassess your other skills and see if there is something you've missed. To pivot does not mean that every week you are doing something new. It is an adjustment that is the result of self-reflection and research. Throughout my career I have been able to continually reinvent myself because I regularly take stock of the market, what is needed and what I'm offering. The more we begin to embrace modification in our lives that leads to evolution, the more access we gain to the power sources that we need to shine.

THIRTEEN:

BANDS: RESTORATION AND RETHINKING YOUR TRUTH

WHAT YOU THOUGHT DOESN'T HAVE
TO BE WHAT YOU THINK. RETHINK.

—Africa Miranda—

BEING TRUTHFUL WITH yourself is a revolutionary act. Careful examination of our life and the life we hope to have, demonstrates that we exist in a space between truth and lies. And while we work anxiously to live up to the idea of who we are in the minds of others, there is a real person, beyond the layers who desires to be recognized and acknowledged as truth. Shedding the layers of expectation to become yourself is an act of great courage and faith. This process begins with the thoughts that you maintain about yourself and ends with countless moments of rediscovery. When all of the sheets are removed, who exactly are you? What is your truth about happiness? How does success look to you in comparison to how the world has defined it? Your classification of success and failure is directly correlated to what you believe your truths to be. Opening our minds to embrace the concept that rethinking what we believe to be true not only about ourselves but about our destinies and the world around us is a surefire way to elevate.

Learning to embrace the art of rethinking your truth as a part of the process can prove to be a powerful way to intensify our power and escalate our purpose.

ASK THE QUESTIONS

THERE ARE TIMES in your life when you question if you deserve better than what is before you. Just because life is going well doesn't mean that there are not higher levels that can be realized. Not one of us is exempt from improvement. The concept STEP UP, is rooted in the consistent quest for improvement and evolution. Consider the following:

- What factors are driving your levels of efficiency?
- What lessons have you learned?
- What more would you like to accomplish?
- What makes you happy?
- What is your biggest fear?
- What makes you feel weak?
- What makes you feel strong?
- What gives you energy?
- How can you bear more fruit from the offering of your time and talent?

There is no way to improve without asking ourselves critical questions about our disposition, wants and needs. Lastly, do know that it is okay to not have all of the answers. Mindset is the name of the game, and as long as you are taking steps in the direction that makes you happy, the details will be revealed in due time. Breaking through barriers requires us to dig deeper to discover the lives that we want, need and deserve.

CHASE THE SUNSHINE

THERE ARE TWO things we should be after. One is happiness and the other is to become someone whom we admire. Chasing happiness, means denouncing the definitions of others and adopting our own. At this stage, we must not only recognize that there is harm in accepting others definition of happiness as our own, but also disconnect ourselves from the crowd so that we can figure out our own. The template of happiness can be used as a starting point of reference but nothing replaces what feels good to our souls. Paying close attention to the moments that our energy increases is key. Our heart has a way of speaking the words that our mouths are in search of. Striving to become someone that we can be proud of means to be happy with the decisions that we make about our lives and those that we make that affect the lives of those around us. The only way for us to emit light is to become it.

RELAX. RELATE. RELEASE.

SIT DOWN. BE quiet. Retreat. Repeat. We've managed to trick ourselves into believing that we'd rather show the world how hard we are working than taking time to actually bask in rest, relaxation and restoration. Even our time spent on vacation is riddled with the work of capturing the right angles to share on our social media platform. Taking time to rejuvenate is critical to our ability to process and plot our next moves strategically. Every entity that exerts energy, must rejuvenate and that absolutely includes you. Digital devices alert us when the battery is low. Likewise, we must step up to recognize the signs of depleted energy stores within ourselves. I used to be part of the "sleep when you're dead" crew but not anymore. I was on the verge of physical and mental burnout after years of "grinding" and "hustling." Now I work hard and rest even harder. Knowing how to avoid burnout enhances productivity. Learning to identify the signs faster and establishing set rituals for rejuvenation is a non-negotiable. We can not afford to the belief that self-care is selfish. To flourish above the fray, we must venture to produce a cache of remedies purposed for revitalization of what is lost through output. Taking time to attend to our mental health is also an integral part of our ability to retreat successfully. Learning to silence our thoughts, calling anxiety by name, identifying the onset of stress and diffusing negative energy make us a force to reckon with. As Whitley Gilbert said in A Different World, "Relax, relate, release." You deserve it.

STOP AVOIDING

YOU MUST GO out and take everything that you believe you deserve. Your purpose won't manifest in silence and it won't make its presence known in the absence of action. The risk takers of the world are the only ones who will truly know freedom. So often, we avoid the tasks that we believe we will not master on the first try. Why waste the time if it's going to be a failure right? Worse that this, many of us (raises hand) avoid tasks because we know we might actually succeed. The fear of success can actually be paralyzing. You can become so accustomed to the safety and familiarity of "almost" that when presented with the opportunity of true success you self-sabotage. Growth only occurs when we push past the fear. Stop running from your greatness, your power, your light. We must do the things that we fear most. We must accept the challenge.

These moments cultivate and stretch our innate capacity in ways unimaginable.

SURRENDER TO THE PROCESS

WE HAVE BEEN conditioned to construct a plan and work it until we succeed. If we don't succeed according to the plan that we devised, we beat ourselves up and discover new lows from which to own anxiety, depression and other feelings that weigh us down. What if we changed our perception of the truth? What if we challenged our perceptions about the definitions of failure and success? Could it be possible that each moment not classified as success according to the plan, is a sign from the universe to change the course of action or to pivot? Sometimes dreams are deferred for a reason. Divine redirection is a part of the process that we must not discount. I fought for ten years to be a singer. Forgoing so many opportunities while I blindy pushed forward, ignoring messages from the universe that it wasn't my true path. I had to step back and realize that it was time to reassess and pay attention to the signs. Surrendering to the process means allowing yourself to be led to your true path, not necessarily the one you see for yourself.

TO THINE OWN SELF BE TRUE

MY BIRTHDAY IS December 24th, and I take time at the end of the year to reflect and better understand my wins and losses. It is also a time for me to be brutally honest about the areas of my life that need more work and to craft a plan to make it happen in the new year. I used to dread my birthdays because I was so caught up in what my life should look like, and because it didn't, I always felt like a failure undeserving of a celebration. Now I try not to get caught up in what *should* have happened and focus on the tangible moments. Rethinking forced me to focus on the truth. Every year of my life there were accomplishments I could be proud of. Yes, we must always challenge ourselves to be better, but we must also make sure that we are seeing the entire picture. What if you don't have all of the things that you want? No one does, nor should we. If we had everything, there would be nothing left to work towards. We are meant to remain in a consistent state of evolution, growth and desire. With growth and maturity, our wants, needs and motivations should evolve. We must work to see what is right in front of us and recognize the nature of our truths. These truths should not be in comparison or a derivative of others. We must discover them for ourselves. Taking this vital step frees you from the consuming need to compete.

CHECK YOUR EGO

THE KEY TO avoiding emotional betrayal is controlling your ego and not letting it be the master of your domain. One of the best ways to center yourself when you feel that you are spiraling is to ask "what is the truth?" Our ego will write a script that says we aren't enough, that we are alone and unloved, that we are being overlooked. The truth is that we are enough and we are afraid, we are absolutely not alone and that sometimes we are passed over because it simply is not our time.

We've managed to trick ourselves into believing that we'd rather show the world how hard we are working than taking time to actually rest, relax and restore. Even our time spent on vacation is riddled with the work of capturing the right angles to share on our social media platforms.

We've embraced being emotionally savage, and we have learned how to avoid everything that makes us vulnerable. Meanwhile, we are becoming a society of people who are the most connected yet the most isolated. Without exposure to the elements, we don't gain the knowledge that we need to weather the storm. If we've embarked upon a journey to be different, then we can expect storms to arrive. We must be ever watchful of our emotions and allow ourselves to experience the fullness of our hearts. In those spaces, we can find some of the most informative and insightful information about what we can become. These times might be uncomfortable for us because we are treading upon new territory. Denouncing what we feel and saying nothing bothers us, diminishes the light established to reveal the path of destiny. We were meant to feel, and we were meant to experience the highs and lows of life. Doing so, gives us power and permission to revel in the fullness of joy. Anything less is emotional betrayal.

FOURTEEN:

BEYOND OUR BORDERS: LEAVING YOUR MENTAL AND PHYSICAL COMFORT ZONE. CHARTING NEW TERRITORY AND GETTING YOUR PASSPORT #LIT

TRAVEL GAVE ME LIFE. AND
IT CHANGED MY LIFE.

—Africa Miranda

A UNIQUE PARALLEL CAN be drawn between seeing the world and your ability to perceive yourself as courageous in it. Traveling to new destinations means venturing into uncharted waters. Amidst the fear of the unknown, we have the potential to channel profound inspiration.

My breath was absolutely taken away when I saw the Sistine Chapel. I have visited three of the seven wonders of the world, including Christ the Redeemer in Brazil, Chichen Itza in Mexico, and the Colosseum in Rome. There is no comparison between seeing these sites and experiencing them in person, as opposed to seeing them in a photograph. Structures that were created hundreds of years ago that still stand today are awe-inspiring. A very undeniable connection can be made between you and the world that has been created when you witness what another human being was inspired to create. These places hold such strong energy and ignite the genius within you.

This spark doesn't only have to come from travel. Mindfulness that allows us to explore the realm of possibilities outside of our comfort zone, is revolutionary. Comfort zones are not just physical boundaries; they also set mental limitations. The element of fear or discomfort that we feel when we experience new moments in our lives ignite a chain reaction that forces us to alter the dimensions of our entire being. We are stretched to accommodate new ways of thinking and a new approach to life. In this space is the opportunity to chase our goals and aspirations. We must learn to be comfortable with the concept of being uncomfortable in an attempt to embody who we want to become and how we wish to be positioned.

THE FABRIC OF YOU

HAVE YOU EVER noticed that people seem a little different after they have had new experiences? The only true way to discover what you are made of is to remove outside influences. As you go about your normal, daily routine, the domination of everything from media to government to those we love, takes over. These factors tend to leave an imprint on our decision making, and they influence our view of the world around us. Invariably, we are being molded and shaped by what we experience. This ongoing process can take a toll on our goals and where we see ourselves positioned in the world. The mounting pressure to fit in and to be a part of what we see around us can have lasting effects and prove to be the culprit that provides a sense of comfort in a safe zone.

Most often, there are two ways to leave our comfort zone. The first is by choice, and the second is by force.

In any facet of life, building up the courage to leave a familiar place is not easy. Paying the deposit to visit a new destination or making up your mind to leave a job that no longer serves you, takes effort. In instances in which we are left with no other option than to engage in new experiences, we can feel powerless. Being relieved of duties from a role in which you served or not being selected for a specific opportunity can be distressing. On either side, the end result of leaving the comfort zone is an unfamiliar experience. Extending ourselves and our psyche beyond the existing borders also means we must reframe the way we define an experience. Experience brings wisdom, and the more you know, the more well versed and equipped you are to broaden your horizons. When you experience something for the first time, you can learn so much about what is on the inside of you. Monitoring your response to certain variables of life and the series of events that unfold, reveals a great deal about you. How you react to new people and uncertainty will hold a wealth of information from which to be empowered. With this information, we have the power to determine what we truly want from life. No other voice should have such power. Seeing the world changes our perspective, but it also makes way for solidarity. Who doesn't need a dose of that? My favorite way to explore a new city or country is to wander, get lost, and find my way back. The same wisdom can be applied in many facets of our creativity and in our lives. You've got to get lost to find yourself!

CONFIDENCE

HAVE YOU EVER watched another person do something while thinking to yourself, that if he or she could do it, you had the ability too? There are people in the world right now doing things that you have convinced yourself that you cannot do because of a lack of confidence or fear. The key to setting foot on new soil, whether in spirit or in truth, is confidence. We must learn to lean and depend more on the imaginary step that we can't view beneath our feet and having the faith that it is there. Confidence comes from believing that life is not set up for us to flounder. We must be insistent upon examining what feels like failure and recognize the difference between lessons that have been set in motion to make us greater versus factors that are meant to destroy us. When we resolve to take a leap of faith, we must acknowledge that whatever happens will result in a learning experience. The biggest shift for me was to start asking "why did this happen *for* me?" instead of "why did this happen *to* me?" Little shifts in perception can produce life altering results. All I ever wanted was to live in New York. Both times I lived here, I complained about everything. It was too cold, too inconvenient and riding the subway is akin to being rolled down the street in a garbage can (yes I'm being dramatic, but have you ridden the subway?!). Let me tell it, my "dream" city was a nightmare. I left New York last year only to return nine months later. In those months, I had a huge professional setback and had nothing but time to reflect on and over analyze my life. New York is never going to change, it will always be what it is...at its best or at its worst. *I* had to change. Why was I being so negative about a city that is full of art, culture, inspiration, and so much life? These are all the things that I love, and they're here. I decided to be grateful that I can live in a city that challenges me the way New York does. Instead of complaining about it, I vowed to come back and hold tight to a grateful mindset. Within months of returning, my life was transformed personally and professionally. Without that setback last year, I never would have done the self-reflection that was needed for me to reach this next level in my life. This city has always tested my confidence and self-worth. I can say that I finally feel like I'm flourishing here and not frantically treading water. I now have a renewed sense of purpose and confidence that I never had before.

ESCAPE BOREDOM STOP COMPLAINING

AT SOME POINT, you must know that if you continue to do the same thing with little to no variation, you will get tired. Who wants to live a life filled with mundane moments? Sometimes, you just have to shake things up. People in different places think, act and conceive differently from you. Exposure to new patterns of thought is a surefire way to channel new adventures. This doesn't mean that you always have to jump on a plane. Something as simple as breaking your normal routine by taking a different route home or going to a different neighborhood for lunch can shake the dust off and give you new inspiration.

As much as you may complain or feel defeated personally or professionally, there is always someone who is less fortunate than you. Life has many ways of teaching us this treasured lesson. If you venture into your backyard or to the other side of the world, an open mind will make you a living witness that there are many disparities in the world. I can't, in good faith, complain about my circumstances after seeing first hand how women across the globe nurture their families with much less. We can always reap the benefits from lessons on grace and humility.

TURN ON YOUR SPIRITUAL WIFI

TRAVELING IS A spiritual experience. You feel connected to the world when you see people getting on a train to go to work, walking the streets of their city, dining in restaurants and living life. You recognize that we have more in common than we are led to believe, and we are so much more connected than we realize on so many levels. The more you travel, the more empathy you have for people. Observing another culture up close is a strong reminder that no matter how different we appear, we genuinely desire the same things in life. We desire to be loved and to have the freedom to be understood and discover happiness. Enlightenment also empowers us to leave judgements at the door. If we can exercise a more heightened compassion for humankind, we can discover an affinity for life.

For me, travel broadens my world view and gives me a deeper reverence for the human spirit. You will smile at someone and not be able to speak the same language, but you can find a way to connect. Those things happen organically because we are all part of a global family, and we have a divine thread that binds us. The more you engage with new worlds, the more profound your connection to yourself and the world abroad will become. The world awaits you

REPROGRAM YOUR BRAIN

YOUR BRAIN REQUIRES exercise in order to function at optimum capacity; it is just like any other part of your body. You're a thinker, a dreamer, and a doer, and those are all action words. Much like our bodies, our brain needs to be pushed to assume new proportions to ensure that we are able to conceive of the abundance that is meant for us. If your thoughts are not consistently aligned with the belief that life has more to offer you than your current situation, no matter how great or small, how can you ever be capable of reaching for more? There are times when we dream too modestly. Dreaming with borders and limitations is a disservice to the fulfillment of the higher calling that we have received. If we want more, we must reprogram our thoughts about what more means and contains. Reprogramming our brain is an ongoing activity. To reprogram does not always mean to erase all that we know, it could mean deepening our learning and understanding of various concepts. Higher thinking is what we are after at all costs. Making decisions for our lives from an intelligent disposition versus one from an emotional stance can assist us in strategically operating for success. As we reprogram our mindsets, another impressive factor to be considered is clarity. With the extreme amount of messaging that we encounter on a daily basis, it is valuable to have clarity in as many areas of our lives as possible. Every facet of who we are and who we are becoming is a work in progress. When we clarify our vision, goals and directions, we can become a more well rounded individual.

REDEFINE LEARNING

LEARNING TAKES PLACE in the fire of what feels like failure. To reach success, you must experience failure. There can be no trial in the absence of error. The way in which you value the acquisition of new information is the "tell all" as to whether or not you will position yourself for the win. Approaching life as if we already have all of the answers creates an environment where purpose can not thrive. When we consistently thirst for the acquisition of new knowledge, we recognize that things will get a little uncomfortable, and that's okay. Living your best life is about remaining laser-focused on the exploitation of new opportunities to learn and grow. Real life goals consist of learning about yourself, people, places and things, none of which can be done in total if you don't find ways to gain access to new people, destinations and experiences. Redefining learning means that we recognize that failing is relative. Consider that feeling that has made you most afraid, that place that you are afraid to go, that step you are afraid to take, this is where you must lean in. Fear is a hindrance and does not allow you to walk in purpose. The very thing that causes you to fear is the very thing you must do. You owe it to your purpose to push past fear. The greatest lessons of your life are positioned on the other side of fear and failure. Push through!

ESCAPE

A VACATION IS synonymous with taking a break from the monotony and putting your mind at ease from all that it is expected to do on a daily basis. Even though the term vacation immediately draws our senses towards visions of distant lands with palm trees and beaches covered in white sand, a vacation can be as simple as an undisclosed location in your city and a cell phone in *do not disturb* mode. Taking the time to get away to relax the mind is still a form of charting new territory. To grow into the new dimensions that a life of excellence will require, you must be willing to find reprieve and rest in unexpected places. Viewing your escape as a part of the process for tapping into your greatness is key. You and you alone are responsible for making these moments possible. You can't afford not to release and exhale on a regular basis. All of the deadlines, emails and texts will be there when you get back. In the meantime, dare to get away. We've been given the gift of life on this earth for a limited time. If we really knew how much time we had, we'd likely not need to be convinced to escape. Prioritize and do it. Now.

THE FINAL SAY

PERSEVERANCE IS NOT OPTIONAL.
IF YOU WANT RESULTS.

—Africa Miranda—

CAVEATS AND FANCY THINGS:
ALL YOU HAVE TO DO IS FLY

TRAVEL FAR. TRAVEL OFTEN.

—Africa Miranda—

WHEN I WAS growing up, I took a ton of road trips with my family from Alabama to Boston. Every year, I looked forward to seeing the many landmarks along the way. I would check them off as we traveled on the almost twenty-six hour journey. My favorite sites included the peach orchids in South Carolina, the cigarette statues in Virginia, and my most favorite was the George Washington Bridge. I always wanted to be awake when we crossed the bridge because the lights of the city were as intoxicating to me then as they are now. My family also loved taking cruises, and these vacations continued to expand my worldview. The love affair with travel that started in my youth stalled in my twenties, but it was reignited when I turned thirty years old.

When I was thirty, I traveled to Mexico with an ex boyfriend. While the relationship left a lot to be desired, he was an avid traveler, and I credit him with opening that door for me again. The next year, I went to Europe for the first time. A few months after returning, I took a trip to Rio de Janeiro, and it would change my life. I define my life by who I was before I took that trip and who I was afterwards. It changed everything. A friend was working there for 6 months and it was basically a trip where I had a place to stay but for the most part would be on my own. I was nervous because there would be no one to pick me up when I landed, and I would have to navigate getting to the hotel and around the city on my own. This was in 2008, so there was no Uber, and I definitely didn't have an international phone plan. After getting help with the ATM I had my *reals* (Brazilian currency) and headed to the cab line. I had done my research so I knew how much a cab ride to the hotel should cost, and I knew that it should be a metered cab. My life as a New Yorker had prepared me more than I realized. After a shouting match with a cab driver who wouldn't turn on the meter, I was able to get in a proper taxi and was headed to the hotel.

After dropping my bags off at the hotel and getting a quick city overview from the concierge, an hour later, I was sitting atop one of the city's most beautiful landmarks, Sugarloaf Mountain. The experience of sitting miles above the city while writing in my travel journal prompted me to realize that I would never be the same. For the next week, I enjoyed Rio as a *carioca*. I hung out at the beach, took the subway (which was MUCH cleaner than New York and easier to navigate. Tuh!), got lost, and on this week long adventure, found myself. Brazil felt like home. Before I arrived, I expected the Gisele Bundchen version of the city. I wasn't prepared for it to be so...brown. My family on my father's side is Cape Verdean, a people who are descendants of slaves and mainly Portuguese colonizers. Afro-Brazilians are essentially the same. Everywhere I looked, I saw my face, my cousins, aunts, my grandmother. It was beautiful, and the way I was embraced by the people during my time there was unlike anything I've ever experienced. I also felt like I was welcomed in a different way because I looked like I was at home, and in many ways, it was home.

In so many ways, my time in Rio changed my perspective and what I believed myself to be capable of doing. I realized that I could do anything, and I was capable of doing something by myself. What if I hadn't taken that trip because I didn't have a friend to go with me? It was in that moment that I realized that if I wanted to go, I should go. The change in perspective ignited a paradigm shift in what I willed to manifest in my life. Once I broke the seal, the opportunity to travel started to come to me with ease. I've now traveled to over twenty-three countries, and while I love traveling with friends and groups, I cherish solo travel and have made sure that it will always be a part of my life.

I had an epiphany that I could create an arm of my brand that explored the vast possibilities of the world through travel. My passion for travel was now a part of my purpose. Instead of traveling and assuming all financial responsibility for doing so, I began to travel and share my experiences in collaboration with brands and businesses. Not only did I not assume the cost but I was being sought out for opportunities that would be financially beneficial for me. Seeing the world in all of its splendor is the perfect way to STEP OUT. Leaving my comfort zone was the absolute best thing that I have ever done to tap into my purpose.

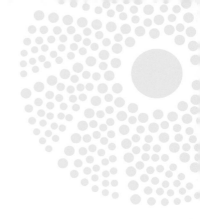

III. SHINE

THE MOMENT THAT I
RECOGNIZED I DESERVED
THE *WHOLE WORLD*, I
MADE THE DECISION TO
GIVE IT TO MYSELF.

—Africa Miranda—

THE FRAMING THOUGHTS

IMAGINE WHAT YOU can and will accomplish when you relinquish your need to be accepted by others. Living life on your terms, your own rules, in a way that works for you is the embodiment of intentional living.

During this time, the dimensions of your expectations for yourself and those around you stretch to new proportions. This mindset commands that you vibrate on a higher level and that the energy that you emit and exchange is full of potential.

When you shine, it becomes unfathomable to turn the light off. You now recognize that under no circumstances should you dim your light, nor will you allow anyone else to do so. The discovery of this form of enlightenment is wealth. To SHINE is to recognize the fact that your light will not burn out; it is replenishable, and your shine is eternal.

What would you do if you knew who you were? How would you live if the shackles of life were removed? One who vows to SHINE, recognizes that limitations only exist in the mind.

To SHINE is to exert every ounce of energy towards divine purpose, without apology. Simply stated, to SHINE is to flourish.

One who vows to SHINE knows that there is no force strong enough to eliminate destiny and purpose.

THE THEORY

OUR LIVES ARE not static, and success is relative. If you are only tied to one vision of what success will look like, you will always feel disappointed. As your life changes, the picture of success must also mature. On a cellular level, our bodies are continuously regenerating over our lifetime. Why is it that we hold on to one vision and one vision only? Why aren't we letting our dreams grow and change? You must be willing to adjust your path to success and be opened to it manifesting in unexpected ways.

CONTINUAL ACTUALIZATION

CONTINUAL SELF-WORK IS one of the most important parts of continued growth. A willingness to do whatever it takes to achieve is paramount, but working to ensure that your goals are met and continue to flourish is just as critical. I like to look at life as a living, breathing Google document. We should constantly be reviewing it, looking for errors, making sure that the words written are clear. It should be the same approach to our lives. You don't miraculously wake up as the best version of yourself on a daily basis. The path to our higher selves involves continuous education, self-evaluation and forward movement. Each "edition" of ourselves should be better than the last.

OPERATING IN TRUTH

THE TIME TO SHINE is directly connected to walking in our truth. From an early age, this can be challenging because we are living in a society in which we are socialized to lie and call it being polite. We lie to protect the feelings of others and to shy away from real issues that we don't wish to address or direct our attention. Being honest is attributed to being critical or unkind. Contrary to popular belief, operating from a place of truth reveals kindness. If we lived in a world that valued honesty, we would position ourselves to be happier, healthier, and more whole.

In a relationship, how many times have you been hurt or disrespected and say that you're "fine?" How many times have you lied to yourself about what you want or how you feel? By repeatedly lying to ourselves and others, we normalize this behavior, and without realizing it, we invite dishonesty into every part of our lives. Reprogramming ourselves to value the truth over everything else means that we have to emotionally clean house. If I'm not fine, I don't say that I am. I've learned to speak up. Walking in truth also means getting to the true "why." When I was being honest with myself, I recognized that some of my anger or resentment, in certain situations, was the reflection of my own shortcomings. It is always easier to transfer responsibility to other parties. Shining our light can only happen when we are striving for truth.

THE ANALYSIS

TO SHINE IS to denounce limitations at every entry point of life. The only valid questions become:

- What do you want?
- Who will you help?
- How will you do it?

Although many would have us to believe that there are more pieces to solve the puzzle, there aren't. To some degree, it is a challenge, on a daily basis, to answer these questions, but their merit remains the same. Every single day there are messages telling you that you are not supposed to be where you are or that you are not worthy of accomplishing what you set out to achieve. To SHINE, you must have strategies in place to silence these voices. You must tell yourself on a continual basis that these messages have not been established for you. They hold absolutely no weight.

Do you believe that some people just don't have it? *It* can be the factor that sets the stars apart from the sky or the secret sauce that results in stardom or affluence. Often referred to as the "it factor," we've been led to believe that some people possess it while others don't. In mainstream media, we've witnessed countless examples of shows that create stages for people to battle it out in an epic moment, attesting to the fact that they should be crowned a natural born star. From reality tv to pop culture entertainment, there is no shortage of rising stars versus those who have fallen or never even ascended. Is this even a real thing? Should we believe that some of us are gifted with abilities and others are not? Are we to put stock into the assumption that we were not all created equal?

Each one of us has been divinely appointed with genius. It presents in everyone in different ways, but it is there. It is important to decipher what messages about your gifts you allow to penetrate the surface. One major difference between those who will walk through life intentionally and touch success is the ability to filter out messaging that is malignant to their purpose. Your filter can keep hope alive amidst what feels like the death of dreams. You can not succeed if your filter is not strong enough to disarm the forces that create doubt, anxiety and indecisiveness about you or your purpose.

Even today, with all of the strength that I possess, there are times when I can still hear the words of the producer who told me I didn't have it. I can be straight with you all. If you've made it to this point in the book, we are family now. While that producer wasn't right, he wasn't one hundred percent wrong. I am not an amazing singer—the likes of which the world has never seen. I am a *good* singer and a strong, solid performer with moments of greatness. I have worked on my craft over the years and I am confident performing on any stage. With that said, my destiny was not to become a recording artist. Could he have shared his critique without being an asshole? Sure, but that pivotal moment in my story was necessary to get me to the life I have now. We can all hear the words of those who meant to break us but never succeeded. We have to shake ourselves out of it. We must engage in those self-talk conversations that lead us to the truth about who we are, our capabilities and the intent behind our actions. You must be your own cheerleader and coach and get yourself back in the game, every time.

I talk in great depth about being truthful with ourselves. I will not say that all of the criticism that I have ever received in my life has been one hundred percent inaccurate. There were times that I could have done more or cultivated my talent differently. It takes hard work to align yourself with honesty, especially when it hurts. These brutally, truthful moments are where true growth happens, and they should not be taken for granted.

THE PERSONAL TESTIMONY

"YOUR LIGHT CAN HELP YOUR
NEIGHBOR ESCAPE DARKNESS."

—Africa Miranda—

MY FAMILY STRUCTURE wasn't a traditional one. My parents separated and divorced when I was very young, leading my mother to pack us up and move from Boston to Montgomery, Alabama where I grew up and consider home. My father was in prison, and most of my early memories are of visiting him there on our yearly family trips to Boston. My maternal great-grandparents and grandfather were property owners and ran several small businesses. I spent my childhood learning how to run a cash register, handle inventory and general customer service. I didn't realize until very recently how much this influenced my journey as an entrepreneur and a creative. I purchased my first home at twenty-two years old. Again, I didn't realize that this was out of the norm because it was what was normal in my family. As much as I now appreciate the foundation I was given, back then I hated feeling different. While growing up, I lived in the rural part of town and never

lived in the same neighborhood as any of my class-
mates. Even though we owned acres and acres of land,
my house was old and looked nothing like the homes
of any of my friends. My mother, grandmother and
aunts were also Jehovah's Witnesses, so I didn't share
the typical southern, Black Christian experience and
couldn't connect with much of the cultural camarade-
rie that can bring. I just remember always wanting to
feel "normal" or the "same." I chased that feeling for
a very long time and became adept at transforming
myself into the version of me I thought would be most
loved and accepted. For a long time, it worked. College
offered freedom from a strict, religious upbringing,
and I flourished. I pledged Delta Sigma Theta Sorority,
Inc., was active on campus, and I was university homecoming queen, which was a real moment at an HBCU.
I was still performing and was very active on campus.
As an adult, I continued to perform in relationships,
contorting myself in the hopes that it would guarantee my partner's love and fidelity. Performing and more
performing.

If this sounds exhausting, it is because it WAS. As I
neared the end of my thirties, I knew I didn't want to
have to perform for the rest of my life. I wanted to finally

just be. To SHINE for me may seem like it has all been professional, but the most happiness I've experienced is found in the light that is shining unapologetically and authentically in me. Initially, our approach to life is because of our surroundings; however, to SHINE, we must take an active approach to getting the tools that we need to change the course or create a new narrative.

SHOW YOUR RECEIPTS

WAITING FOR AFFIRMATION is the same as waiting for someone else to give you permission to live. To SHINE is to take responsibility for affirming yourself at all times. It is very rare that we say that we are proud of ourselves. We don't own our accomplishments as deeply as we should. We instead wait for someone else to tell us that we did a good job. This is not about being boastful or arrogant; it is about assurance. For a long time, I would hesitate when people would ask what I did. When I answered, I was fearful of sounding boastful or vain. Even now, I have anxiety about promoting so many projects or announcing accolades on my social media feed. We are all working. Hard. We deserve to shout our wins from the rooftop and we shouldn't have to wait for someone else to tell us we are killing it. Shining feels amazing, and you should let yourself enjoy it. Seeds long planted are bearing fruit, and it is time to enjoy the harvest. Affirm yourself right now!

POWER

FOR MOST OF my life I did not feel powerful. As women, I think we do a great job of performing, and this was a skill I picked up very early. We can look like we are walking in power but live quite the contrary. True power is in how kind and loving we are to ourselves. There is no power in working yourself in the ground for everyone else and suffering with little to no benefit for our toil. We shouldn't be martyrs to our dreams. Saving our families, friends and communities at the expense of our body and spirit has to stop. There is nothing powerful in putting yourself last.

To SHINE means viewing moments of self-care as preservation as opposed to selfishness. We can be of no service to others or our purpose if we are not of service first to ourselves.

ASKING FOR PERMISSION

WHOM SHALL WE ask for permission? There are no gatekeepers of your destiny. Why do we need someone to tell us that the way in which we desire to live is okay? The fact that you were given the desires, talents and gifts that you were given is permission enough. Asking for acceptance or permission to walk in purpose is like requesting entry to a door for which you are holding the key. When I changed my mindset of constantly needing to be chosen and recognized, I found so much peace. For years I wore what I like to call the "cloak of desperation." I was ensconced in my neediness and desperation; I took it everywhere I went. When we want something so badly, we don't realize how the energy we're giving off can actually repel those around us. I had to release the white-knuckle grip on what I thought my life was supposed to be and surrender to the larger destiny that was waiting for me.

After Stepping Up, then Stepping Out, Shining is inevitable. The future that seemed hazy is now a much clearer picture. Opportunities and recognition you once prayed for are now a regular occurence. You no longer need to ask for doors to open; you are being welcomed and holding opened doors for others. I know this may sound very "unicorns and rainbows", but I know what it is like to sit in your lowest moments and not know if you can make it out. You are meant to be whole; your life has value, and you will walk in the sun once again.

FIFTEEN:

IF NOT NOW, THEN WHEN: DOING WHAT YOU'VE NEVER DONE BEFORE

TO BE A DIAMOND, YOU MUST
BE WILLING TO GET CUT.

—Africa Miranda—

ALTHOUGH WE ALL have a different approach to life, the process to enact transformative results is the same. Nothing great happens in our lives without great risk. You must walk on the wild side, daring to do what you have never done and venturing into the unknown. If you dream of something-anything, you must find a way to do it. We fear that failure or loss will become a part of our destiny when we take risks, but nothing could be farther from the truth. When we exploit potential, we either win opportunity or wisdom, and both are valuable. The only decisions that we can deem right, are the ones we make. Placing purpose on hold will not work. Once you have started on this path, it will gnaw at you like an itch just out of your reach you need to scratch. Just as you need air, food and water to sustain your physical body, fulfilling your purpose is necessary to feed your mind and spirit. Your desire to succeed must trump all fear of failure.

KNOW THAT YOU ARE WORTHY

YOU ARE ENOUGH. From this point forward, forget the words of anyone who has told you that you are too little or too much. For every flaw, there is a beautiful story that makes you valuable. What you have to offer the world is specific only to you. Walking in that truth and owning all that has occurred in your lifetime give you a perspective from which to teach, build and nurture. The world is gifted by your presence and your energy.

You must know that right now, in this moment, the world is blessed by you. You don't have to look like anyone else, dress like anyone else or become a watered down version of yourself. To SHINE is to walk, with your head held high, in appreciation of all that you are. Enough apologizing for who you are because someone finds something offensive or not suitable for them. Dim your light for no one.

It is also important to be mindful that your value is not tied to what you can do for others. You are valuable because you exist. Greatness and transformation manifest when we learn not to sit on or suffocate our gifts. The more you share them, the more light your life gives to the world.

USE YOUR OIL

AFTER YOU HAVE connected with your purpose and made a strategic decision about who and what you want to be, you must become a lifelong student of your gift. The more enlightenment that you can attain, the better. Learn the history of what you are opting to do. Discover who the trailblazers are and study their stories. It is likely that you will find similarities between yourself and those who have come before you. No concept, idea or pattern of thought is new under the sun, and this works in our favor. We can add our touches of innovation to change the world for ourselves and others. Your research will also lead you to an inevitable wealth of knowledge to counter any obstacles that you may face along the way. Someone, somewhere has traveled the road that you are attempting to navigate.

When you see someone that is doing what you want to to do, pay attention. Success leaves clues. If the person whom you are observing has discovered progress or profit, you'd best believe that there is a trail of breadcrumbs leading to how they got to that point. It is up to you to discover the leads. Become a super sleuth, if you have to, but don't start from scratch. There is an entire world, filled with information. Imagine how much farther ahead you will be when you discover that hints and clues to your success have been left behind by others. While being inspired is key, duplication is never the answer. The very thing that is unique about you, is your secret sauce, or oil as I call it. You don't need anyone else's influence because yours is the most important ingredient needed to complete the recipe for your dreams.

MAKE CONNECTIONS, NEVER COMPARE.

YOUR PURPOSE WILL require you to engage with like-minded people who dare to dream as profoundly as you do. These individuals will serve as sources of inspiration and motivation to push the envelope. In many instances, you will see the value in stepping your game up and taking your brand to the next level. Anything worth having will not come easy, but if it is for you, it will be yours. Have confidence that you can perform in excellence and that you deserve a seat at the table, even if you have to create it yourself. The key is being strategic about each move that you make. From the people that you establish bridges with to the places that you frequent and the daily activities that you engage in, everything must align with purpose.

While you are making these connections, you must never forget that engaging in comparison can throw you off your game and have you questioning your journey. You can't run a race when you are looking right and left. This is advice I too must heed. Some days I scroll down my feed, and I find myself questioning why I wasn't chosen for certain opportunities or why this person seems farther along than I. I am extremely competitive. Competition is one thing, but comparison is another. You should know your market and your peers, but don't compare your day to day with others. Everyone is not the same. Check in and see what's going on and engage organically, but set limitations that prevent you from becoming a lurker of someone else's life. Develop a close relationship with the "mute" button. It does not serve your strategy well to focus on what anyone else is doing.Your ultimate strategy is to be you and to make the associations between where you want to go and where you are currently grounded. A woman with a plan is a woman chasing purpose.

BE INTENTIONAL

HAVE YOU EVER heard someone complain about needing more hours in the day? Increasing our levels of intentionality is a surefire way to maximize the twenty-four hours that we do have. Intentional living yields results, because we begin our day with the end in mind. There is no limit to the action that we can take to be intentional. This can be done with the words that we speak, the places that we frequent, the people that we speak to and of course, the energy that we allow to radiate from and through us.

When we are intentional with our words, we say what we mean and mean what we say. This ignites a breeding ground for effective communication. When we speak clearly to others, they become clear on what we aim to accomplish. Clarity alleviates wasted time in misunderstandings that soak up valuable time. Intentionality in the places that we frequent means that we are only present in places that serve us in some form or fashion. It can be a community space in which we volunteer our time or talents, the grocery store to purchase foods that yield healthy choices or places to socialize with people who speak positively to us and fuel our fire. Intentionality will save you from being present in places that you are not appreciated.

Intentional living means that you recognize the power of your energy and that you are not willing to allow it to be used in ways that don't serve you or your purpose. Creating a haven to provide a barrier against the outside world is important. Clearing your space of clutter, bringing in living things like plants and fresh flowers, burning sage and candles - all are great ways to honor your living space.

RING THE ALARM

IF YOU ARE going to chase a dream, you must do so with your entire being. You must be totally committed; it is not enough to just say what you do, because we live in a time where the proof is in the pictures. To establish yourself as the person of choice in your industry, you must SHINE. The only way to become a gleaming example of who people should call if they are looking for your presence or service is to establish yourself as the expert. This means that you command authority because you are well versed. No one cares about process and how the magic happens, people want to know that you can get the job done. Being the authority establishes leverage and makes you the person of choice, which adds value and validity to what you are doing.

Don't be afraid to tell people what you do. In fact, tell everyone. Study your craft without ceasing and be the most knowledgeable in your industry. Build a community of people who believe as you do and look to you for the facts, trends and innovations in your designated arena. Be the first to know the new developments and share the news. Document yourself doing what you say that you do. Get references from people who have approved your work. Create an online presence that shows evidence of your work. Be visible to those that are in search of you.

Once I knew how I wanted to present my brand to the world, I began to strategically position myself for opportunities that were conducive to my goals. I began hosting and creating live streams to show and demonstrate my work. I invested in cameras, created and directed my own photo shoots. Consistent action over time is a no brainer when your intent is to SHINE.

GET NOTICED.

THE FIRST STEP to getting noticed is separation. Flying under the radar does not position you to

SHINE. You must find ways to separate yourself from the pack. What makes your approach to doing things different? What message does your brand establish and how are you solving people's problems? If you want to be great or recognized, people should not have to look hard to find you. You should be easy to locate when they are ready for you to be of assistance to them through the use of your gifts.

I have made my intentions clear about how I want to be known. I feel that it is important for me look the part, sound the part, and live the part. The most empowering aspect of it all is that I am myself. My brand is a true extension of me. I don't have to be one person in public and someone else behind closed doors. The authenticity is what keeps me close to the community of support that I have developed. Also, keep in mind that the types of opportunities that you encounter will change. Be prepared. There is a leveling up that happens in your life as you move towards higher heights. New things will be required of you, and you will be expected to innovate to stay above the fray. This ties into you ability to be proactive. When you live a proactive existence, you start to see the profit from your work. One of my special "shining" moments was when I was invited on my first large press trip to the South of France with Kia Motors America. I was speaking at a conference that Kia was sponsoring and connected with the brand there. Within weeks, I was extended the invitation to go on this once in a lifetime experience. To receive an opportunity like that was mind blowing. I knew was deserving of it because I had done the work necessary to position myself for recognition. During the prior year, I had worked tirelessly to build a brand that yielded an opportunity. This offer and many others since then haven't just happened. They have been the result of a strategic planning.

That trip also became the inspiration for releasing my second product for my company—Beauty by Africa Miranda. It was a new extension of my existing brand but a proactive approach to how I could grow my base and offer a product to solve a problem for the community that I have established.

RINSE AND REPEAT

GOT CREDIBILITY? NOTHING makes you SHINE more than demonstrating that you can consistently yield results. Consistency is the name of the game.

Trust is what is established when you do what you say you can do on a continual basis. This alone sets you apart from the crowd. Consistent action brings about results on a perpetual basis. When we demonstrate ourselves to be of good integrity, we have the power to dominate on every level and pull ahead of the pack as the number one contender in whatever it is that we seek to do.

It is not enough to do what you say you are capable of doing a few times. To SHINE is to recognize the necessity of perseverance. The race is won by those who understand the importance of optimizing their potential. The more you do something, the better at it you become. More people will seek your services because you deliver better results. I always say that if you are going to be a bear, be a grizzly! Don't only strive to be *your* best but strive to be *the* best. Competition should not be feared when you operate in your purpose.

SIXTEEN:

INSTINCTS, INTUITION AND INTELLECTUAL PLEASANTRIES

I DON'T BUILD WALLS: THEREFORE,
I AM NOT CONFINED BY THEM.

—Africa Miranda—

ONE SUREFIRE WAY to know that you are in a position to SHINE is when you find yourself thoroughly enjoying and being stimulated by active and passive knowledge. For many, it is not enough to use brain power to get through the day. Those who like to fly above the radar, recognize that knowledge is literally the pillar from which every foundation is built. Those who love to witness changes in processes and make things better, rule the world. The thinkers, analyzers, innovators, problem solvers, and creatives are all a part of the divine plan of excellence. We are conscious beings, and we are greatly fulfilled from inventing and shaping our world. Those who don't find joy in these activities will be managed by those who do.

MIND + MATTER + LOGIC = FEELINGS

IN THIS LIFE, we must work to understand our feelings and the role they play in our lives. Allowing ourselves to feel is to experience the fullness of life. Allowing our feelings to take the lead however, cancels logic and our ability to make sound decisions. As creatures who are conditioned to feel, it makes total sense that we often find our emotions taking precedence over logic. Engaging in activities that reprogram our approach to what happens all around us and within us can change the flow of energy and the course of actions that we take in a given scenario. We train and strengthen our bodies and we must do the same for our minds. One great exercise is to spend less time replaying events in our heads. We have a tendency to overanalyze things to the point that all logic is thrown out the window. Instead of focusing on problems, remain fixated on solutions to enhance your quality of life and achieve your goals. Another way that we can manage our emotions is by properly classifying our feelings. How many emotions can you identify by name? Far too often, we find ourselves feeling things that we can't identify. We must learn to label every feeling as the first step towards conquering it. When we can distinguish our feelings from logic, the victory inside our minds can be won.

DISCOVER INNER PEACE.

DO WE EVER really find inner peace? I don't believe that there is one true definition. It can hold a different meaning for each of us. It is something that we must never stop working toward. To conceive it as a final destination sets us up for failure. Instead, we must strive to have balance in our thoughts and our emotions that keeps us actively in pursuit of internal peace. When asked, I never say that I have attained inner peace. Instead, I continue to strive to live my best life, and I work hard to be as happy, centered and grounded as possible. I stopped striving for perfection long ago; it doesn't exist. Even on your best days, you may be carrying some baggage. When all is right with the world, you may be struggling internally with a decision that needs to be made. To channel inner peace, give yourself a moment to connect with your inner voice. We are over inundated with messaging, triggers and information; we simply need tools to deal with the highs and lows. Learning to accept what is can always yield tremendous results in our ability to be at peace. How often do we stop to welcome elements or scenarios of life just as they are? We don't have to change everything. We are not responsible for everything. Taking ownership of too much can lead to being unnecessarily overwhelmed.

SELF-COMPASSION. GET SOME.

AS YOU SHINE, you will need a friend. It is often lonely at the top. Look no further because the person who understands you best is the reflection you see in the mirror. The higher you aspire to go, the more you subject yourself to pressure. During these moments, not only will the expectations of you increase, but your expectations for yourself will also increase. In all things, you must remember to be kind to *you*. Even when others are not, you must serve as the gatekeeper for your heart and soul. We don't even allow ourselves to enjoy some of the greatest moments of our lives because we are busy attending to how others will experience the moment. Sometimes you have to forgo the photo for Instagram so that you can live and breathe the moment for yourself.

There is a great contrast that occurs when we consider how to be good to ourselves. To the world, you can appear to have it all, but simultaneously you may be suffering in silence. The hard truth is that no one really cares. It is all the more reason for you to care about yourself and your well-being. Your job is to never cease in finding moments that bring you joy. We must never stop believing that life has a sweet moment that awaits us. We must never forget that compassion is not a luxury that is reserved for moments when we are deserving, compassion is an act of care that we can't afford to live without.

CLAP FOR YOURSELF.

I'M ON A mission to impress myself on a daily basis. After you have completed something that you set out to finish, there is power in celebrating yourself. You deserve to be applauded. Let's be honest, the fact that you are still standing after what you have managed to survive deserves recognition. Like most, I am very hard on myself. We accuse ourselves of not doing enough, not achieving specific milestones by certain ages in life, and not being who others need us to be in every capacity requested. I don't think that we realize how much we subscribe to society's definitions of success, as opposed to our own. Life never presented us with an instructional manual or guidelines that specified when we deserved to be praised. Why do we demean our power by waiting to achieve a standard that is imaginary to begin with? Stand up, brush your shoulders off, and clap for yourself. The only sound of applause that you need to await should come from your own hands. When you know that you've walked in purpose and power, clap harder, clap louder, throw your hands in the air if you have to. You deserve to be praised!

SURVIVAL OF THE FITTEST

YOUR INSTINCTS HELP you to survive, but when given proper attention, they help you blossom. When you recognize how to SHINE, survival mode will be a thing of the past, and all emphasis will be placed on transcendence. If your instincts have been divinely appointed to save you from harm, why not use them? Consult them at all times. Your instincts can drive you towards your greatest ambition. What are ways you naturally excell? Think of skills you have that are above average without even trying. They can become the compass when the map of life appears to be a puzzle. Instincts, at their most basic level, are our body and spirit's natural response system. It will take some time, but start listening and let them guide you. Learn to trust them. The more you lean on them and hone them, the stronger they will become.

TRUST THE DIVINE CONNECTION

INTUITION, OR DIVINE messaging, is present in all of us. No matter what higher power you believe in, there is an undeniable connection between humankind and the universe. Intuition has been given to us as a source of protection and guidance. While it is ever present, over time I have learned that intuition doesn't just kick in. The messages only make themselves available when your mind and heart are opened to what they have to say. By practicing gratitude, meditation, and other means to keep the channel open, we will never miss out on the information we need at the right time. Just like with your instincts, you also have to learn to trust your intuition. Everytime in my life that I have blatantly disregarded what I knew deep down to be true, the results have been disastrous. Conversely, when I've trusted the connection the results have been mind blowing. The first time I sat with the publisher of this book, Ardre Orie, I knew that she was someone I could trust. Specifically, the message I heard was: "This woman is going to change your life." Not all moments will be this crystal clear, but once you are tapped in you will be able to discern even the most subtle communication. Your intuition is what led you to Step Up, then Step Out, and will continue to guide you as you Shine.

SEVENTEEN:

NO PRESSURE: DENOUNCING THE WORLD'S NOTION OF WHAT YOU SHOULD BE. CREATING YOUR OWN

I LOOK MY BEST WHEN I AM MYSELF.

—Africa Miranda—

HOW MANY TIMES have you been told to be strong in your lifetime? I can almost guarantee that you have lost count. I most certainly have. As a woman, especially a woman of color, I receive messages on a daily basis that emphasize how strong I am supposed to be on any given day. Moreover, while, it is without question that strength is a part of my being, there are days when I feel weak. This is true for each of us. It baffles me that somehow, we've adopted the narrative that we don't get days off. Like, whoever said that allowing ourselves to embody the fullness of our emotions on an off day was a crime? In complete transparency, I no longer force myself to squeeze into the stereotypical space that dictates my internal messaging.

Strength has never been a word that I have gravitated towards. For me, it is a concept that is overdone. It is not something that is a part of my lexicon. I don't have any passionate thoughts about strength. I see myself as resilient. I am more into resilient. Resourceful. Hardworking. Intuitiveness.

Resilience to me is about taking what life throws at you and continuing to move forward. Recoil governs that we find ways to persevere in the face of obstacles and doubt and factors that you have to overcome. In the midst of it all, I've always found a way to rise like the phoenix from the ashes. I would say that my career has been about resilience or resiliency and innovation.

For me when I hear strength, it reminds me that I'd rather be discussing evolution. I don't think that there is a lot of conversation about evolution. Our ability to pivot when necessary and to innovate whom we believe we are becoming and should be speak more to me about progression than any notion of strength. Survival in this world is about denouncing what we are told and creating what we will. You can be strong by just surviving. The more interesting conversation is about innovating.

YOUR BODY. YOUR MIND. YOUR DESTINY. YOUR CHOICE.

SOMEWHERE IN YOUR thoughts, you dreamt of whom you would become. That image is ingrained in your psyche. Day to day life and the perils of the world could make you forget but holding that image close to your heart is not optional. There is no way to be whom you want to be, without a vision for your life. The only person that you are responsible for becoming is the person that you have chosen to be. You don't owe it to anyone else to live up to a specific standard or any given level of existence that has been predetermined by anyone else. Don't get stuck between who you are and whom you want to be. Constantly evolve. Find ways daily to get closer to that image. Why have a vision board that must be left at home, when you can envision your life in your heart and take it with you everywhere that you go? The truth is that everything you want to be, you already are when you believe.

REMEMBER WHO YOU ARE.

BE YOU. DO YOU. There are specific components of who you are that should never be compromised, nor reconstructed. Your values and ethical beliefs should never be adjusted to make others feel comfortable in your space. As long as who you are does not endanger others, you do you. Bloom. You are the flower in the garden that was divinely appointed to grow and to prosper. Regardless of what is happening around you, it has very little, if anything to do with your purpose. Your vision for your life and your existence has already been ordained. The farther that you get away from it, the more restless you become.

Conforming to societal standards places a burden on who you have been called to be and all that you have been slated to accomplish. So many have spent so much time walking outside of the realm of their purpose while trying to fulfill an imaginary image to appease others.

There is no reason to work hard to impress people who will not be there when you fall. To this same end, the people who recognize your brilliance will be there to cheer you on and encourage your ascension. In the realm of your SHINE, you won't even feel comfortable when you are not yourself. Walk in greatness and make no apologies for it.

YA HEARD ME?

HAVE YOU EVER stopped to consider that the universe will only respond to the beliefs that you own about yourself? You do realize that society profits when you don't believe in yourself don't you? The more you attempt to alter yourself with solutions that only make concessions for your lack of confidence, the more someone else profits. Why should you allow the world to dictate all that is inside of you? Since when did your purpose deserve to be bound by societal stipulations? You are significant. Your life matters. You belong. Let no one tell you anything to the contrary. If you don't stand up and affirm yourself, you will wait for an eternity for others to do so. The more you believe that you are worthy and that you are deserving of miracles, the more they will be attracted to you. This is not to say that you don't have to do the work to achieve, but amplitude is yours. Do you know what you do well? Have you taken the time to decipher what you offer the world that it just can't live without? Your abundance is rooted in your ability to leverage your greatness. The world is your stage, get up and dance!

CLOSE YOUR EARS. CLOSE YOUR EYES.

IT IS SO amazing how the world tells us to chase success and status when neither of those things will bring us joy deep down on the inside. If you only subscribe to the messaging that the world yields, you will always be a victim and not the victor.

Stop believing what you hear and what you see. Even salt presents as sugar. We were meant to breathe life into the world. We have not been called to wait for an opportunity to fall from the sky. We have not been exposed to light to walk around with darkness in our hearts. True happiness will only be realized when we solidify our purpose in service to others. The world tells us to be self-centered and compellingly vainglorious. And while I wholeheartedly support believing in yourself beyond a shadow of a doubt and putting yourself first, there is more to life than that.

We will reap the greatest harvest when we understand that there is joy in giving of ourselves to make the world better.

Being of service to others spreading love and demonstrating humility through acts of service directly connect us with purpose. And it is possible that you might not get as many "likes" or "follows" while doing so but the greatest of all joy will be discovered in your heart.

WHO DID YOU SAVE THOUGH?

OF COURSE, YOU must be the first to place emphasis on the cultivation of your life. No one will do it for you. Never forget to keep that same energy when it comes to helping others. Stop believing that everything is about you. It's not. At the end of the day, you have to look in the mirror and ask yourself what you did that made a difference in the lives of others? And I'm not talking about massive feats like raising a million dollars to save the whales. While I do believe that every cause has merit, you can make a difference in your everyday walk. Did you smile at the person you passed on the street? Did you take the time to encourage someone through text or a quick call? Did you give the gentleman on the corner a dollar because you knew you could spare it? Possibly you paid for the coffee for the person behind you in line at Starbucks. Whatever you can do to value others, do it. That speaks more profoundly about whom you are becoming. As much as you put yourself first, you must also consider how you can impact the world around you.

SHHHHH!

I KNOW YOU have heard the saying: "there is nothing new under the sun." And it may be true that ideas are recycled, let's be clear, you are not. You have not been here before. This is not your second trip around the universe. That means that you are unique. There is not another you. The world has not yet experienced your greatness. How could you mistake the opportunity to showcase all that you are destined to be with mediocrity? You were made to dazzle as the sun does. Don't think of compromising or belittling yourself because someone has proclaimed that you are not enough or that you don't fit a certain standard. You don't have to. In the moments when others tell you that you don't belong, find ways to create your own space. When the world and the people around you attempt to impose their processes of thought on you, silence them at all costs. This is not your messaging. You weren't meant to be cast into the shadows. You were meant to SHINE.

CHANGE.

WHY IS IT that when someone tells us that we have changed, it has a negative connotation? Who should remain the same? Forever? How would being the same speak to the many lessons that life has taught us? How would finishing the same way that we started attest to the journey? There is no merit in remaining the same. In fact, to remain the same in the absence of growth is to die. We must never stop yielding to the process of life happening within us. We must never stop believing that life has more to offer. We must never stop chasing our dreams. We must never stop aspiring towards greatness. We must never cease to believe that there is genius inside of us that should be unleashed. Whom shall create doubt and fear and uncertainty within us? Why would we ever allow anyone to have that much power over our lives and our destinies? The woman who grows is one who hastens towards change. Revise, innovate, advance, convert, transition, remodel, pivot if you must, but whatever you do, change.

EIGHTEEN

REDEFINING YOUR TRIBE

SURROUND YOURSELF *WITH* PEOPLE
WHO ADD FUEL TO YOUR FIRE.

—Africa Miranda—

W HEN TALKING WITH friends, how many stories do we hear about people who have changed? It is even possible that if you were not present, the conversation was about you. As we mature, it's understood that all friendships aren't meant to last forever. We begin to understand that people's visions for their lives expand. The capacity for the people in our lives changes. This is a part of life, but it does not mean that all relationships are meant to come to a screeching halt. I don't believe for a second that the value and emphasis that we place on relationships have faltered, even in the age of social media. Those who genuinely wish to connect and thrive together, do. Relationships that are built upon mutual exchanges are alive and well. The key is cultivating time, energy and space to engage in upliftment. If you can't rely on your friends to "gas" you up, who will? They should be able to rely on you to do the same. The benefits of friendship are priceless when everyone builds together.

Ascension also comes with a heightened sense of discernment that keeps you informed as to who you should keep in your circle and who you should keep at arm's length. Everyone does not mean you well, nor does everyone mean you harm. Consider what you bring to the table to positively impact the lives of others, just as much as you consider how someone can make your life better. The exchange is key for anyone who intends to SHINE. Wherever you intend to go, do realize that everyone will not be able to travel alongside you. Only those of like minds and similar will and fortitude will be your teammates as you venture towards your purpose. It is also important to note that there will be some destinations that you must travel to alone to receive your blessing. Those who support you will cheer you on as you go. While it is not necessary to enlist a "yasss crowd," it is imperative for your tribe members to see the potential in you and you in them. Your life is your circle, and the people that you spend the most time around dictate what will become of you. If you are the most accomplished, driven and purposeful person in your circle, how will you continue to rise? You need to be around people who are pushing, competing and fighting to get to the next levels in their own lives. Now, that is motivation! Your tribe should consist of those who are just as driven as you are; some might be more driven than you. I want to spend my time around people who are pushing so hard that I have to fight to keep up.

MAKE AN EFFORT.

FORMING A TRIBE is not easy. It definitely evolves over time but still requires your action and attention. We can be so caught up in what we have unfolding in our daily lives that we don't stop to make time for organic exchanges. I've made an effort to meet women and men whom I admired. It is important to me to surround myself with people that I can learn from. I am not the most accomplished in my circles, and I am extremely proud of that. If everyone you know is asking you for advice, who can you ask? Those who SHINE recognize that who you know actually *does* matter. Your tribe will evolve, and so should you. As the stakes continue to rise, your levels of intelligence should continue to soar, and the levels of burgeoning success should be inevitable. This can't happen if you don't take time to step outside of your comfort zone to meet those whom you admire. Are you unsure of a way to connect with them? These days social media is the best virtual networking party there is. See if your faves are on social and follow them. Like/share their posts and where appropriate, comment and engage. If they have an email listed in their bio, you can also use that as well. I challenge you to use your better judgement because there is a fine line between online admiration and stalking. There's nothing worse than being blocked by someone you admire. I was able to connect with one of my favorite authors, and I thank Instagram. We've now developed a connection offline, and I'm so glad that I took the opportunity to contact her.

USE AND BE USED.

WHY HAVE WE villainized being used? Taking time to meet and exchange with those that you are inspired by and to connect on a genuine level is an extremely positive act. I think that the lines get blurred when people make requests with no intent to give in exchange. People that vibrate on higher levels recognize their value and know without question what they bring to the table. You should be getting something from people, and they should be getting something from you. If the relationship is not pushing you forward in some way, why are you there? We should all be using each other to learn. We should all be using each other to grow, and dare I say that there should be some narcissism involved in the exchanges. People like to say that narcissism is bad. I personally think a little dose of narcissism is necessary to keep the train moving. If you don't think you're the best thing since sliced bread then who will? The whole element of narcism is that you should embrace the notion that "I'm the shit." You should be looking in the mirror on a daily basis and reaffirming your worth. Why wait for others to do so? You be the first. Be the first at everything. Be the first to want to win. Be the first to put yourself first. You should want people to choose you first for friend-ships and for opportunities. Who is working hard to be in third place? I surely hope that we have no desire to be in the third position. If you are working for first and you are behind Beyonce and Oprah, then you are not in bad company. You will always be right behind someone that is amazing if you work hard. Find a way to unite with those people and push harder than you have ever pushed before. Never shy away from build-ing bridges and alliances with the best.

DO THE MATH.

LET'S ADDRESS THE fact that there is greatness available to everyone. Not everyone is willing to take the steps or do the work that is required to reach their full potential. That's okay. It's not our place to decide how far or how fast another person should run. With this concept in mind, we must also embrace the fact that holding on to every relationship is not feasible while journeying towards purpose. Holding to those who don't desire or aspire to go farther is equivalent to holding on to the anchor at the bottom of the sea, waiting to reach the top of the water. You can't rise if you are holding on to the weight. Relationships that do not fuel your fire are anchors. And while they can help you to remember who you once were and keep you grounded in your beginnings, they may not lift you any higher. I'm not afraid to say that it is fine to distance yourself. You owe no apologies for being selective in how your time is spent and with whom you spend it. Take a moment to analyze which relationships are worth their weight and which are not. Never forget that we now have social media that allows us to stay in contact and celebrate each other without bearing the brunt of the weight of relationships that no longer serve us. You can stay in touch, but you can filter the energy that is being drained. This includes family, friends, and anyone else that you are considering for status in your tribe. You can love people, but they do not have to be a daily presence in your life. Friendships are simple arithmetic. If the effort and energy don't add up, the value is negative. As our wise big sister, Jada Pinkett-Smith, once stated, "You can love them from over there."

LET IYANYLA DO HER JOB.

I GET SO caught up in seeing a person's potential. I can see so many possibilities when I look into the faces of people that I know and many that I don't know. It's as if I can see the menu of gifts and talents given to them, even when they can't see them in themselves. I believe, with my whole heart, that we are called to help others along the way in every way that we can. Prior to understanding how purpose works, I would often fall into a trap of trying to help everyone. I would create or find projects to do for the sake of collaboration. There are people that I have given advice at numerous times, and I'd likely do it again. What I failed to realize was that many people are fine where they are. You can't love people into their potential. You are not Iyanla, you can't fix anyone's life. You have one job, beloved, and that is to assume responsibility for fixing your own life. Let Iyanla do her job!

As much as you think you will pull others up by teaching and preaching and paving the way, things might not go as you had hoped. This does not mean that you should not lift others up, but being strategic in how you do so is key. When you are driven, you always want to bring everyone along, but you can't want success for others more than they want it for themselves. One of the most powerful things that you can do, in addition to mentorship, is light a path and serve as a shining example of what can be done. You are the light, go be it!

DITCH THE PLUS ONE.

HAVE YOU EVER gone to a social gathering alone and been pleasantly surprised by the new people that you have met? There are times when going alone opens possibilities that you had not otherwise considered. When you are not attending to the needs of others and ensuring that people are comfortable in a given setting, your hands are no longer tied. You are open for new opportunities without restriction. Sometimes you just have to go alone. Creating distance is not always about others as much as it is about the changes that you need to make to reach the next level. You must constantly ask yourself what you need to be doing to evolve in the way that you desire. There must be a constant evaluation of the steps that you need to take to put your purpose in motion. As you become more purposeful, you have no choice but to be more selfish. Your destiny requires all of your attention. It can seem cold or a little callus, and maybe it is, but it is also the truth. You have to fight ferociously for you, your happiness and your peace. There must be standards and strategies in place to alleviate anything that impedes your progress or your peace. That means that everyone who compromises them, in any way, must go. Getting to this point can be very lonely, and sometimes it means stepping away from people. Remember that this journey is about you. As your life changes, so shall your circle. This is not to say that things will always be this way but do find a way to prepare yourself for seasons of isolation. During those moments, you must place your ears to the ground to hear the divine calling and messaging from the universe about your next steps. These are moments that you can't afford to miss.

GIRL, EVOLVE.

MY CIRCLE TODAY is by far not the same as it was even five years ago. Even so, I still have many friendships that have withstood the test of time. When I look back, I don't think that I actively went out and said "I have to make new friends." They evolved as I evolved. When I first moved to NYC, I made a close set of friends that eased my transition, and they have remained constants in my life for the past sixteen years. They provided the security and foundation I needed to take the earliest steps of this journey, and I know I wouldn't have survived many of the ups and downs of life without them. When I left New York and moved to Atlanta and started performing, I found a new creative family. These extremely gifted people pushed me in music, art, and in fashion. With every turn, I have fallen into new circles, and I am thankful that God brought me them in my life. It is definitely harder to make new and substantial connections as you get older, but if you keep yourself open, it can happen. Continue to do the work to seek people out whose interests align with yours. These are the building blocks of constructing a tribe. In the end, those that desire to win, evolve and win together.

NINETEEN:

THE LOST ART OF TRANSFORMATION: REINVENTING YOURSELF, UNAPOLOGETICALLY AND WITHOUT NOTICE

AND AT NO POINT IN LIFE, SHOULD YOU
EVER CONSIDER REMAINING THE SAME.

—Africa Miranda—

NEVER STOP REINVENTING yourself. Period. She who resolves to SHINE is a living, breathing testimony to the power of reinvention. To grasp the concept of reinvention, you must first understand who you are and that there are levels to your greatness.

It is not possible for you to grow and still be the same person that you were a decade ago. Growth demands that a new layer be removed and that a new surface be revealed. We define reinvention in a variety of ways, but the concept itself is simple. With the acquisition of new knowledge, we are made new. With every new destination we explore, we are made new. Reinvention is all about expansion of dimensions. It should mean something different to each of us as we set out on our individual paths with the common goal of a life of purpose. Most importantly, we must be open to seeing ourselves through a variety of lenses. We must embrace the concept of our lives in different formats. Failing to change as the world around you changes, means being left behind. If there are two things that we can be certain of, they are chance and innovation. The people that are the most fulfilled and successful have not remained the same, nor should we. If you're dragging your feet, life has a way of forcing our hands to do so. Why must we be forced into evolution? The more we embrace change, the more in sync we can become with what happens next.

GAME RECOGNIZES GAME.

WITH AGE COMES wisdom. Life has a funny way of preparing us for the unknown. The gift that we must learn to enjoy is that life leaves traces of insight along the way. The more we pay attention, the more easily we recognize patterns from which to improve our approach and response to what happens all around us. It behooves us to adopt the concept of reinvention as our own. We must also recognize that life's template is revealed during unforseen moments. Essentially there are three moments in time that force us to reinvent ourselves and turn over a new leaf in our lives. Although we never want to think about tragedy, it is one. If not in our own lives, we can watch the effects of tragic events in the lives of others. When life sweeps us off our feet in ways unimaginable, we are never the same. Some find strength in transformation, and others discover their passion amidst pain. The art is in our ability to weather the storm. Another moment of life induced reinvention is when we are hurt by another person. From failed relationships to disappointments in humanity, we, in turn, become more of who we wish to see. The best lesson I've learned from the trauma I've experienced in my life is that I have a blueprint for what not to do. I strive to never make anyone feel small, dismiss their feelings, or have them feel ignored. We have the power to become the change that we desire to see in the world. The last instance that we are forced to reinvent ourselves is when we are sick and tired of being sick and tired. Believe me, you'll know when you are really done. When you are called to greater, you will develop a sense of boredom with your current life. I can tell a major shift is coming in my life when I am literally physically uncomfortable. I can't get settled, nothing "feels" right, and it's as if there is an electric current tingling right below my skin. The only way for me to get relief is to sit still and listen. In those moments, I usually know what changes I need to make, but I have been procrastinating. Those who SHINE are never quite satisfied as they know that there is always more. We will benefit greatly from listening to the messages, signs and signals that are divinely provided for us and embrace change. Reinvention is inevitable, and greatness requires our undivided attention.

KEEP THE TAB OPEN.

YOU SHOULD NEVER be out of ideas or dreams. When you are alive and living in the present, the list of things that you want to do should be so long that it is overwhelming. The goal is not for you to accomplish it all; the goal is for you to evolve towards those things that rise to the top of your bucket list. Waking up in the morning should be a gift, and the opportunity to engage in something that you love becomes the present. Setting your sights on accomplishing new things will require you to shed fears, doubts and past inhibitions. With every passing day, you must see yourself as worthy of doing new things, hard things, things that you don't see others do everyday. It is up to you to challenge yourself. The fountain of youth that everyone chases is not found amidst complacency. One of my biggest inspirations is Angela Bassett. Do you think that her waistline is snatched because she sits in the house on a daily basis allowing life to pass her by? Absolutely not, she continues to take on new roles with a variety of depth and dimension. She is diligent about her health and fitness, and as a result, she has made sixty the new thirty! She hasn't found the fountain of youth, but she has mastered the art of reinvention. Another example of reinvention is Jennifer Lewis. She can be seen on any given day, doing a high kick with her heel to the heavens. She decided to challenge herself and go public with her battle with Bipolar Disorder. In doing so, she opened the floodgates for candid conversation to heal the masses and herself in the process. Examples like these have given me the inspiration to keep going. I have had so many creative "lives," and I continue to grow and evolve because I haven't let myself become static. From singing, modeling, acting, reality tv, to now entrepreneur and even author, all of these stages required my vulnerability and taking a chance. Some paid off more than others, but all were necessary to get me to this moment. Reinvention is about going there to save yourself. In the process, you will also save others.

REIGNITE AN OLD FLAME

NOTHING SPEAKS OF intention and vigor more than going for something that you didn't get the first time. Let's be clear, just because you didn't get what you set your sights on the first time, does not mean that it is not for you. We must continue to allow our definition of failure to evolve. Setting your sights on an old goal is just as noteworthy as setting your sights on a new one. Until you realize what you hope to accomplish, all bets are off. You are free to exert everything inside of you until you feel satisfied, and it's no one's business. No matter what happens, you set the energy in motion for the universe to conspire with you towards what you want to see manifest in your life. There is nothing more powerful than setting a target and aiming for a bullseye. The best part of reigniting an old goal is that you have more experience than when you first initiated effort towards it. This means that you can change your strategy; your approach is more seasoned, and you can even move with a little finesse. There is no time like the present to chase the things that you believe will change your life for the better.

SEE YOU AT THE CROSSROADS.

EVEN WHEN YOU have managed to discover your SHINE, there will still be moments when you long for more from life. Don't apologize for being ambitious. The climate of your life will enter into a new season, and change will become a part of the plan. What feels like a crossroad is your season of reinvention. Deciding to leave Atlanta in 2014 and move back to New York was that moment for me. I had people question the move, and I even questioned myself. Things were going very well for me, and to the outside world, it seemed crazy to leave a city where I was experiencing a level of success. I couldn't explain it, but I knew that there was more for me and that I needed to go back to the place that challenged me the most to find out what it was. When this happens, this is where you have to dig in. There will be a moment of reckoning that whispers in your ear, and it will tell you to choose yourself. These moments are jewels of a lifetime and are not to be denied or ignored. During this season, you must assume every opportunity presented to test the waters. Dare to go deeper in understanding, in truth and in trial and error. The only person that you must be better than is the person that you were on yesterday.

GO PUBLIC

REINVENTING YOURSELF IS a journey, and it most certainly does not happen overnight. The more accountability measures that you put into place, the more likely you are to achieve. Consider making your new mission public. You've watched people announce to the world something major that they are going to do and then leverage the power of social media to document the journey. A great example and everyone's favorite friend on Instagram, is Will Smith, and his "I'm turning 50" birthday challenge. Since his entrance to the world of social media, he has taken every viewer by storm, mastering the platform almost instantly. He proclaimed that he has always been afraid to jump out of an airplane and that turning fifty also meant that he needed to overcome fear. He made an entire post dedicated to how fear is paralyzing and that he did not want to align with anything that could impede his progress. On his fiftieth birthday, I'm certain that he will show the world what it looks like to overcome fear in a major way, and we will all take notice. The strategy is brilliant.

No matter what, when you make your quest for reinvention public, the prospect of turning back fades away. So up the ante and tell the world your goal and jump!

GET COACHED.

IF YOUR GOAL is to SHINE, it is evident that you have no interest in being average. That said, you need people in your corner who can push you to your fullest potential. If athletes can benefit from the oversight and tutelage of a coach to break records and make history, then we can take a page from their book of excellence. I've worked with vocal coaches, physical trainers, taken branding courses, even classes on how to improve my Instagram feed. If there's something I don't know or I need to know to take my life to the next level, I will work incessantly to get the knowledge. Even with all of my studying and reading, there comes a point where I need expert instruction. From showing you ways to harness your inner strength to strategies to yield the best results, it is possible that the right coach can take you farther than you had the ability to go on your own. Coaches aren't reserved for a specific area of your life, and they come in all genres. Whether you desired to take your financial management or your physical fitness to the next level, you can change the trajectory of your next move by adding another layer to your support system. Working with a coach can also keep you accountable when you feel that the uphill trek is too much to endure. It can also prove to be an instant confidence booster as you push past plateaus. Life coach, trainer, accountant, tour guide, teacher, you name it; there is a professional who is ready, willing and able to focus on your reinvention.

TURN BACK THE HANDS OF TIME.

WHEN WE ARE young we are always in such a rush to "grow up." Younger me had very grand plans, okay?! As we get older, life starts to chip away at our dreams and childhood visions for our lives, leaving us yearning for the carefree days of our youth. I don't know that we are getting "old" as much as we are buying into safety and calling it maturity. I feel younger today at forty-one than I did at twenty-five because I am no longer bound by what society says I should feel or want. I am experiencing life on my own terms, and the freedom has taken a weight off me that I carried for much of my adult life. A pleasant by product is that, as the years go by, not only do I feel lighter, I look more youthful, and I feel more energetic and strong.

There is one key question that you must ask yourself on a daily basis: Am I where I want to be?

If you can answer "no" in truth, then you have established a clear case for reinvention. Reinvention can and should occur everyday. We are presented with new opportunities on a daily basis, if we are willing to embrace them. The only way to truly invest in your future is to continuously shape what it looks like. We use the notion of finding ourselves as a crutch, while we should be placing much more emphasis on *creating* ourselves. A change of habits for new results, a change of scenery for new perspective, or a change of people for new connections form the ingredients for the recipe of change in our lives. Make yourself who you want to be. Letting go of the need to be understood is key while on a mission to reinvent yourself. Your vision and mission must be crystal clear to you. The rest of the world can

catch up in due time. Your vitality becomes most appar-
ent when you sustain over time. Reinvention is the key
to staying power. We do not become old when we seek
first to become better.

TWENTY

PASSION + PURPOSE = PROFIT

*WHEN PASSION AND PURPOSE ARE
ALIGNED, THE SKY IS THE LIMIT!*

—Africa Miranda—

I HAVE NEVER LOVED math. There was a point in school where the numbers turned into letters and I could never seem to quite catch back up. What I do appreciate about math is that it is constant. Two plus two will always equal four, four plus four will always equal eight, and so on. In my life I'm constantly presented opportunities and for the longest time I would find myself doing things I didn't really like or ultimately weren't that beneficial. Little did I know that math would be my saving grace. There is a life equation I use to help guide me when I'm making decisions:

Passion + Purpose = Profit

Like any good math problem, let's start by breaking down the parts. I first ask myself before starting any new project or activity if I am passionate about it. Does it evoke a strong emotion? I don't waste time anymore on things that don't move me. So if your answer is "yes," then let's continue to part two. Is this something that is in line with your purpose? You'll notice that this equation is at the end of the book because if you have yet to identify your purpose, you'll be hard pressed to make decisions that fully align with your goals. Knowing if something is in line with your purpose is key, because being passionate about it doesn't mean that it is worthy of the majority of your time. Many of us waste time on passions that would better serve us as very fulfilling hobbies. To successfully complete this equation, your passion AND your purpose must align. If they do, you will always have a profitable outcome. Financial reward is amazing, but isn't the only way to define profitability. When using this equation successfully your rewards will also include the acquisition of knowledge and the reward of pouring into others.

FINDING YOUR PURPOSE

SHOW ME A person who has not searched for their purpose. We all search aimlessly, only to realize that our purpose has been with us all along. The first step in this process is learning how to quiet the voices. Have you taken the time to ask yourself what you want? There is something that you are doing right now that yields an unsolicited response from others. How are you helping other people, without even thinking about it? How can you transform the world or the community that you frequent? All of these questions lead you to purpose. As Auntie Oprah states, "Purpose is right under your nose." The direct line to purpose is discovered when we hone in on how we help others. If you begin with what you like and love and enjoy, you will also find your passion. To SHINE, you have identified your purpose and are in a place to consider how your purpose can work for others and you. When you discover what moves you, your next order of business is to find out how it can touch others. Creating opportunities and opening doors for yourself is one thing but executing this same energy for others is the next level.

DON'T GET BURNED

PASSION LEADS US to the most powerful questions about love. In movies it brings star crossed lovers together and in life it has even driven people consumed with passion to kill. Passion is the fire in our bellies that forces us to make decisions. Passion can create anxiety that forms an ulcer powerful enough to eat us from the inside out. Passion with no direction can be blinding and many mistake it for love, when in actuality it probably hovers on the spectrum a little closer to obsession. We need to have a zest for life and a drive to succeed, but we must make sure that we are the ones in control. Always refer to PX3 (Passion + Purpose = Profit) if you are unsure what moves to make. Passion can be intoxicating and if you're not careful some of your passions can take you off course. I've found the best way to manage my many passions is to indulge them within reason. Music is my greatest passion, however it doesn't line up with what I feel is my life's work. I still perform on a regular basis and keep a musical circle so that I am always feeding that part of myself. Your passions are what make the difference between living and merely existing. Honor their place in your life and you will be fulfilled and balanced.

COUNT YOUR COINS.

YOU WILL PROFIT from anything that you are passionate about if you exert the energy to cultivate it.

You have to ask yourself if what you are doing will add value to the life of another person in some way, shape or form? It is imperative that we value and measure profit in many different ways. Profit is not reserved only for monetary confines. Redefining reward is a powerful act. If you are changing lives, your gain can be in the results. Profit can be calculated by the impact. You must also consider the increased levels of fulfillment that you experience while making a difference. Sometimes you need your soul to be fulfilled. Sometimes, you need to know that because of you, there is good in the world. We do still need money to live and I do admonish you to collect all your coins. Just because you are a creative doesn't mean that you can't be good with money. We are also meant to build a financial legacy. You may be shining bright, but you still need the lights on. Set reasonable rates for your work, prepare a proposal and ask for a raise at your job, stop procrastinating and release the product you've been sitting on. Shining is an action word. It is not enough to know your worth, you must demand it.

BE PREPARED TO PAY A PRETTY PENNY

PAY ATTENTION TO the moments when your energy increases. Your internal compass will spin out of control when you are operating on purpose and in purpose. Your cup will runneth over, and you will experience gratification at the highest levels. Amidst all of the glory, your purpose will require guts. It is not possible to fulfill purpose without pain. Your passion and your purpose will help you to discover profit, but also cause you to pay for its benefits. Purpose will cost you some nights of sleep, relationships, pride, and the occasional blood, sweat, and tears. There will be times that you have to toss your penny into the wishing well and hope for the best. You can take comfort in knowing that your purpose will not lead you astray. Whatever mountains that you have been called to climb, are meant for you to enjoy the view from the top. It must also be considered that your purpose is often only visible by you. Don't fret when it appears that loved ones, confidants and friends are not in alignment with you. You were called to do this work because you have been given the tools to do so.

RECALCULATION

WHAT ARE THE results that you seek? Do you want to be remembered for your genius? Do you want to impact the world positively? Do you want to save someone? All of these questions lead to answers rooted in profit. Sometimes, you might not have finances to support your actions. This is a hard truth. What you are most passionate about does not always profit in the way that you conceptualized it. This is not to say that you are on the wrong course. In this same consideration, it can be a tough life to live on passion alone. Passion does not pay the bills. The high can be high, and the lows can be very low. For me, this was the case. When I was chasing passion, it was hard to sustain. It was an ugly truth, but my truth nonetheless. PX3 showed me how to calculate what actions were moving the needle financially and what actions just felt food in my soul. If you have a lot of things that you are good at or things that you like, how do you decide what to choose? I was at a place that I was getting a lot of opportunities, but they were not all profitable. In the midst of all of this, you don't have time to dissect each opportunity, because you don't want to miss anything. If you are at a good place in your journey, don't waste time.

The equation gives you a way to see if what you are doing works.

PERSEVERANCE IS NOT OPTIONAL.

IF YOU DON'T push through life's obstacles, nothing transformative will happen. That is not how life works. Even if you have discovered your purpose, it is not possible for you to wake up in the morning with the expectation that your opportunity will rise to greet you. Opportunity, purpose, passion, nor profit manifests that way. You must chase what is inevitably chasing you.

I had to do the work to see what my purpose was. Pushing past opportunities that seem hard, pushing body mind and spirit, pushing past forks in the road is all a part of the process.

You have a decision to make. Do you stay with what is comfortable? How much do you desire to be recognized for your greatness? You can't straddle the fence. At some point, you have to decide how you want your life to look. Ask yourself if you want more? If the answer is "yes," go get it. Your answer has to be "yes," every single day of the week. And after you answer "yes," you must then heed the call to do the work. People that are fine where there are are not getting up an hour earlier to chase dreams. People that are fine where they are are not your people. If you want more, the answer is already yes. You know what you want, but it will not come easy. Most people give up at the cusp of their breakthrough. You must be relentless in your pursuit. You must not take "no" for an answer. You must push harder than you did yesterday. If you want it as badly as you say you do, you will not lose.

THE EQUATION NEVER FAILS.

THIS EQUATION, PASSION+PURPOSE=-PROFIT, never fails. The results are the results. When you align yourself with your purpose and thrust your energy and gifts and talents toward the things that you are passionate about, you *will* profit. There is no magic formula for success, and our paths towards it are as varied as our fingerprints. This is the beauty in the construct of purpose. The final destination is a journey and what a revelation it becomes when we finally recognize this. The time that we spent fighting in a restless state to determine what we should be doing, transitions into purposeful living and moments filled with strategic, sound decision making. This is the crux of what it means to SHINE. Passion+Purpose=Profit.

TWENTY-ONE:

THE ART OF STORYTELLING: DEFINING YOUR NARRATIVE, YOUR WAY

THE FREEDOM TO TELL YOUR STORY,
IN YOUR OWN WORDS, IS THE
GREATEST POWER THERE IS.

—Africa Miranda—

STORIES BREED HOPE for the possibilities that life can bring. Stories help us to discover a part of ourselves and to heal from past trauma and hurt. Stories help us to know that we are not alone in the world. Every face has a story, and every story deserves a platform to be heard. There is no shortage of how we can share our stories or the benefits that can be received by them. If we examine our them, we will gain hope and insight as to the patterns orchestrated for our lives. Our stories make us wiser and more attuned to our purpose. There are times that we don't recognize that we have control over how our stories are offered to the world. Instead of allowing others to dictate what is said about us and how our lives are presented, we must learn to become the voice that speaks for us. We must take ownership of our narratives and walk in our truths.

My time on reality television taught me the immense power in controlling my narrative. After that experience, I never allowed anyone else to speak for me ever again. The sense of freedom that I gained taught me a great deal about myself and helped me to plan for my future. There are so many elements of our lives that we are unable to control, however, our narrative is not one of them. Tell your story and set your soul on fire.

STORIES BRING PEOPLE TOGETHER.

NOTHING HELPS US to discover commonality like a good story. Stories appeal to our emotions and tug on our heartstrings. When you harness the power of your story, you have the power to assemble the masses. Finding the key elements that speak to a targeted audience can make your brand legendary. Live-streaming allowed me a safe space to open up Your story reveals your approach to life, the obstacles that you have overcome and the moments of truth that make you who you are. Your story has the power to connect people even in words unspoken. When we hear the ways in which the lives of others have been impacted, the traumas and trials that they have experienced and the good times, we discover emotional ties. The truth is that we are all more connected than we know. Our stories become the proof that we were never intended to attempt life on our own. Every fiber of who we are, unraveled in truth is an opportunity to understand ourselves and each other better.

EACH ONE TEACH ONE.

THE BEST TEACHERS are those who are storytellers. The more you share, the more you leave lasting impressions of your odyssey. The good, the bad and of course the ugly of your trek, can shed light on situations and circumstances that can be avoided. Part of our earthly duty is to help others be fruitful. There's not enough time for everyone to make the same mistakes. Your story can prevent others from making choices that won't serve them. If you failed, you could instruct someone else on how not to do so. If you've succeeded, you can show another the way. You can't sit on all of the glorious information that life has taught you. You can tell about the loss and disappointment that you overcame and the moments that revealed the power you possess. Someone out there in the universe needs to hear from you.

BUILD YOUR LEGACY.

CONSIDER YOUR LEGACY to be a house on top of the hills, standing as a pillar of excellence and hope. The foundation for your legacy will be constructed with the bricks of your life. Every brick represents a part of you. If you don't assume ownership of the building process, your house is sure to crumble. The only way to own your process is to stand firmly in your truths. When you own all that has happened to you, no one can challenge your evolution. In many instances, people try to remind us of who we once were, when we profess to have grown. There can be no power possessed by others when you legitimize your journey. Building your legacy means to stand firmly in your truths. Embracing your story is the most profound practice of self-love. We all have a chapter that we cringe at the thought of being exposed to others, but we must never forget that those same chapters are the ones that can inspire and save lives. We live on through the love and kindness that we share with others, the work that we create, and the stories that we leave behind.

SILENCE THE NAYSAYERS.

I'VE HEARD IT said that "we're all bad in someone's story." This is definitely an accurate statement. We can't be everybody's hero. For those that wish to tear you down, because they can't be you or because they don't want to see you thrive, defamation is an option. We've seen countless examples of people's character attacked, and credibility questioned to create distrust in the minds of onlookers. Whether you are famous or an everyday hero, you must be prepared for attacks on your greatness and gifts. The one thing that no one can take from you is your story. Your truth belongs to you and is a living, breathing example of who you are and what you stand for.

TELL THE TRUTH ACCORDING TO YOU.

IN YOUR LIFETIME, there will be several different stories told about you. Not every version offered will be in sync with your truth. It is imperative that you be in the driver's seat for what the world will know about you and your legacy. There is not a person on earth that can shed light on your truth the way that you can. People may think they know what you have been through, but they have no idea. There are personal struggles that you have kept to yourself and moments that you felt like giving up but didn't. Being vulnerable and sharing my uncomfortable and embarrassing moments has been so cathartic. There were even moments with this book that I hesitated. Ultimately

I knew that by continuing to share my story would provide a bridge for someone else to do the same. Your journey will inspire others but only when shared with the emotion and passion that only you can provide because you were there. You lived it. You should document your greatness. Your life should be the truth according to you.

THOU ART LOOSED.

IF YOU HAVE ever felt bondage in any form, the act of telling your story is the key that unlocks the chains. No matter how far we go in life, we will inevitably experience pain. Chances are that we have locked the pain away in a compartment and thrown away the key. Your scars are reminders of the times that life attempted to break you. Your survival is a testament to the fact that it didn't. You are free because you endured. Survival is not something to keep hidden. Some people are comfortable sharing every moment of their ups and downs, while for others like myself, waiting to share until we've endured the trial is preferred. There is no correct way to tell your story. When and how you choose to share is entirely up to you. It is to be shared with the purpose of inspiring others and setting them free. You are a living, breathing testament to the fact that there is hope and that we should believe in the more that exists.

COMMEMORATE THE WINS.

I'M GUILTY OF having a great win and moving on so fast to the next project that I forget that anything good actually happened. I realized that it was hard for me to celebrate my success, because I still felt inadequate. I know that I am not alone. Time after time, you have been victorious, and you deserve all that is to come. You must not allow your triumph to go unnoticed. You have a responsibility to tell the story about the mountains that you climbed and survived. We all need to be reassured that victory is a real thing. We need to know that there is good in the world and those good things are on the horizon for those that reproduce positive energy. Not only is telling your story good for others but it is also good for you. We all need to be reminded that we've won. Your good fortune was not a fluke. If it has happened once, it can most certainly happen again. It is beyond important that we take note of the transformative power that has been a part of our lives. We must learn to own it and walk in the realm of possibilities at all times. Telling our stories allows us to relive moments of recognizing and ignite the same power that was used to be victorious. Memories that we breathe life into create legacies of truth and excellence that we revisit when we need motivation time and time again.

THE FINAL SAY

CHOOSE YOU. FIRST AND ALWAYS.

—Africa Miranda—

CAVEATS & FANCY THINGS

ALL MY LIFE I've felt different. Even as a small child, it was as if something just didn't quite fit. It was as if I was a character in a story playing a version of myself, but not truly me. I learned early on to keep my dreams and real thoughts to myself. After a while I hid them so far away I almost wasn't able to find them. Through much trial and error I found my way back to myself, and most days I feel as if I'm still peeling back the layers to reveal new skin. Freedom is a process. A lifetime of dimming your light can alter your reality. The mind and body adjust to functioning on a lower level. But in the quiet moments a voice still speaks to you, urging you to take the smallest of steps. Thankfully I listened to that voice. Have you listened to yours?

I didn't want to leave this earth without knowing that I tried my hardest the be the best version of myself I could be and lived life absolutely the way I wanted. I've tried to be kind, thoughtful and honor the gifts and access that I've been given. This book truly is my gift of thanks to every person who has been a part of my life in the physical and virtual realm. I see the comments, DMs, emails and the through line is the same. So many of you want to know how to get to the next step. It has taken thousands of words, but it really all boils down to this: use your voice and tell your story. The mere fact that you've purchased this book means that you're searching. (It could also mean that you are my family or a good friend and I'll take that too!) In all seriousness, everything you want you can have if you remain open to new possibilities. I can't promise that this book will grow your email list or your followers on IG, but what I can guarantee is that after reading you *will* start to ask the right questions, you *will* start to move in the right direction, and you *will* lead a more full and beautiful life.

It is time to make a choice. It will mean leaving behind many things that are familiar and safe. The journey will require more of you than probably anything at this point in your life, and the reward waiting for you will be just as large. Choose freedom, choose power, choose YOU.

V. EPILOGUE

YOU ARE MEANT to be the light in the darkness that illuminates a path toward prosperity for others. Your experiences have prepared you for this pivotal moment. Every trial and tribulation that you have overcome serve as proof of all that you are. I can assure you that your best days are ahead. There is greatness available to you if you are willing to take the necessary steps toward your success. You are not too late; you are not too old. It does not matter how much of any given resource that you have, you are worthy. The vicious cycle of complacency must be destroyed at all costs. Stop questioning the voice in your head that demands more. Stop waiting for the right time and permission. Now is your time and your access has long been granted. The universe is just waiting for you to catch up!

Life and the universe have more to offer you. Do you believe this to be true? Will you do the work to shape your destiny?

Your life is a manifestation of your ability to STEP UP, STEP OUT, and SHINE.

STEPPING UP requires you to do the internal work in preparation for transformation. There can be no change outside without first tackling the inside. Stepping OUT is all about action. At this time you are taking tangible steps to transform your life. It will be visible to those around you and you will start to experience quantifiable results. Your ability to SHINE is all about evolution and manifestation. Prepare for accolades and dreams coming to fruition. Also during this time, maintenance and the reproduction of positive energy are essential. Shining is your harvest time.

Step Up, Step, Out, and Shine, my mantra and strategy for a purpose driven life, is my greatest gift to you. I hope that you will be inspired and challenged to harness your light, recognize your power, and transform your life.

Your higher self is waiting.

WITH LOVE & LIGHT,

—Africa

VI. POSTSCRIPT

THE WORLD TELLS us to fight for balance. I say, let's all stop fighting for balance and tip the scale. You have been called to do more than just live. You have been called to change the world. Your purpose does not deserve to wait another moment. There is nothing ordinary about who you are, and there are no limits on what you can become. Your only limitation is you.

It's time to eliminate everything that no longer serves you.

STOP:

- Asking for Permission
- Being Complacent
- Being Reactive
- Just Existing
- Hoping for Good Fortune
- Overindulging

START:

- Creating Your Own Rules
- Filtering
- Valuing Your Time
- Valuing Yourself
- Opening Your Mind
- Opening Your Heart

The end goal should not be to find balance or perfect harmony as much as it should be to discover power in all things. It's time to reclaim your time, your energy and your perception of who you are. Reset, refocus and STEP UP, STEP OUT, and SHINE!

THE AUTHOR

A DYNAMIC SPEAKER, ACTRESS and media personality, with distinctive style and quick wit, Africa Miranda has become an in-demand beauty expert, on-camera talent and host. Whether she is visiting exotic locales, partnering with major brands like *Refinery29, Macy's* & *Kia Motors America,* or sharing her take on hair trends and celebrity style, Africa brings her brand of accessible glamour to any setting. A trusted voice in the digital space, Africa has been featured in *Vanity Fair, Upscale Magazine,* on EBONY.com, BET.com, and multiple major publications and outlets.

Africa's next chapter places her squarely at the intersection of two of her favorite mediums. Her highly anticipated first book, *Step Up, Step Out, and Shine* will be released this fall. A guide to tapping into the light within, Africa shares personal insight and welcomes readers on a journey to becoming their higher selves. She is also back on-screen as the host and executive producer of *The Africa Miranda Show* - a weekly lifestyle web series created in partnership with Facebook Watch. Africa can also be found weekly giving her take on socio-political issues and pop culture as a guest host on "Listen To Black Women," a web series co-produced by MadameNoire.com and HelloBeautiful.com.

Africa can also now add "beautypreneur" to her list of growing accomplishments. Her beauty and lifestyle brand *Beauty by Africa Miranda,* marries her love of travel and her extensive beauty industry experience. Each product or "beauty souvenir" is inspired by a specific stop on Africa's travel journey. The first two offerings, the Facial Elixir (Brazil) and Luminous Body Mist (French Riviera), have garnered rave reviews and have been featured on *Yahoo Style & Beauty,* BET.com, and are fast becoming cult beauty favorites.

Currently residing in New York City, Africa was born in Boston, Massachusetts, of Cape Verdean descent. She grew up in Montgomery, Alabama, and is a proud graduate of Alabama State University.

WWW.BEAUTYBYAFRICAMIRANDA.COM

CONNECT WITH AFRICA MIRANDA ON SOCIAL MEDIA

W: WWW.AFRICAMIRANDA.COM

E: INFO@AFRICAMIRANDA.COM

IG: @AFRICAMIRANDA

FB: /AFRICAMIRANDA

TWITTER: @AFRICAMIRANDA

CPSIA information can be obtained
at www.ICGtesting.com
Printed in the USA
LVHW060850181118
597207LV00026B/482/P